1996

Studying America's History

To 1877

Studying America's History

To 1877

Thomas R. Frazier

*Bernard M. Baruch College
of the City University of New York*

THE DORSEY PRESS
Chicago, Illinois 60604

ISBN 0-256-03546-6

1 2 3 4 5 6 7 8 9 0 ML 4 3 2 1 0 9 8 7

Preface

STUDYING AMERICA'S HISTORY is intended to assist you in mastering the materials presented in *America's History*. Each chapter in this guide corresponds to a chapter in the textbook and is based entirely on the information found there. If you use the guide conscientiously, you will be able to understand the major issues explored in the text and will have achieved an appropriate level of comprehension of the essentials of American history.

Each chapter of the guide is divided into several sections:

1. *Outline and Summary.* Following the outline of the textbook, this section summarizes the major aspects of the chapter. It provides a brief review of the topics covered and allows you to recall quickly the basic elements of the chapter.

2. *Essay Questions.* These questions require you to review the material presented in the chapter and organize it according to the thrust of the question. This exercise will assist you in analyzing and interpreting some of the major issues covered in the textbook.

3. *Identifications.* Listed here are several important persons, books, ideas, expressions, groups, events, and so on, that are mentioned in the chapter. You should be able to tell what the name or expression represents and to indicate its historical significance.

4. *Primary Source Analysis.* This section refers you to a specific primary source reprinted in the textbook. The questions provide guidance in understanding the language of the selection and in interpreting its significance.

5. *Map Exercise.* Most chapters of this study guide contain an ex-

ercise based on a map that appears in the textbook. The questions in this section assist you both in the process of reading a historical map and understanding the content of the specific map selected.

6. *Illustration Analysis.* Most chapters in this guide include an illustration analysis. Using specific pictures reproduced in the textbook, the questions in this section provide insight into details of the pictures that you might otherwise overlook. An exercise of this sort can help train you to analyze other illustrations, both in the text and elsewhere.

7. *Figure Analysis.* In some of the chapters in the guide, a Figure Analysis replaces either the Map Exercise or the Illustration Analysis. In these cases, a specific graph or chart in the textbook is presented for analysis. The questions provide assistance in understanding both the material presented and its historical significance.

8. *Chapter Context.* Each chapter of the guide concludes with a brief passage that reflects the continuity of the textbook by placing the chapter in its historical context, reminding you of what came immediately before and what follows.

For assistance in preparing the materials in this study guide, I would like to thank my colleague, R. Jackson Wilson of Smith College.

Thomas R. Frazier
Bernard M. Baruch College
of the City University of New York

Contents

1

The Expansion of Preindustrial Europe

OUTLINE AND SUMMARY

I. Traditional Agricultural Society

A. The World of the Peasant

Most of the people in preindustrial Europe were peasants living in small, isolated villages. They had to work long and hard to eke a bare living off the land. The annual pattern of their lives was dependent on weather and geography. In the north there were hard winters and a short growing season; in the south there was a long growing season but debilitating heat. Mortality was high, with extremes of climate and infectious disease the major causes. Periodic holidays—the onset of spring and the completion of the harvest, for example—were marked by boisterous merrymaking. The land was controlled by the church and the aristocracy, and the peasants paid for the use of the land in produce or in service. The nobility had access to the wider world of Europe and the possibility of an education, while the peasants toiled endlessly, without hope of advancement.

B. The Religious Ethos

The Roman Catholic church provided a unifying theme for European society. The church claimed total authority over the lives of its adherents. In order to strengthen its hold on the peasantry, it sanctified the preexisting holiday calendar and provided a spiritual interpretation of widespread customs. All of the events taking place in human life could be explained by church dogma, and apparently miraculous occurrences were commonplace. In order to make its position in society even more secure, the church ordered Christian nobles to drive the unbelievers out of the Holy Land and to punish heretics with death. The intense conflict over religious ideas in the late Middle Ages had a significant impact on New World exploration and settlement.

C. The Price of Survival

The violence that stalked Europe in the preindustrial period contributed to the strict hierarchical organization of society. Families were patriarchal, with married women having few rights of their own. Property was almost always passed intact to the eldest son. Marriage was often delayed until property was inherited, and more than 10 percent of adults never married. Landless children sometimes worked on their family's farm, but others became part of the wandering poor. Made fearful because of widespread violence and early death, the society took a rigid stand against change. It was out of this kind of culture—patriarchal and conservative—that the earliest European settlers of the New World came.

II. Commerce and Conquest

A. War and Trade

Warfare and trade went hand in hand in preindustrial Europe. Marauding nations, first from the north and later from the Mediterranean, sought to spread their influence and power and, in the process, opened up trade routes between East and West. The superior technology of Moslem and Oriental cultures was brought to Europe and adapted to new purposes. This intellectual exchange opened up a new era in European culture, with the emergence of humanistic philosophy and art. The "Renaissance" led powerful nobles to ally themselves with the emergent merchant class to counteract the influence of the traditional elite of European society—the papacy and the agricultural aristocracy. Prince Henry the Navigator of Portugal was the first to use the new knowledge to find direct trade routes to the East, thereby avoiding North Africa and the eastern Mediterranean, which Moslems controlled. Following Henry's successes, Dutch and Portuguese merchants established trading posts in the Far East. Spanish rulers, seeking to participate in this new merchant venture, financed a voyage of discovery by a Genoese sea captain, Christopher Columbus. Columbus sailed to the New World, thinking until his death that he had found a direct route to the Far East.

B. *The Conquest of the Native American Civilizations*

When the Europeans "discovered" America, there were highly developed Indian civilizations in Middle America—Aztec, Mayan, and Incan. The Spanish *conquistadors* made short work of these societies in their search for gold and glory. Hernando Cortes conquered the Aztec empire with the help of tribes whom the Aztecs had ill-treated. Simultaneously, Francisco Pizarro defeated the Incan empire of Peru, and by the mid-sixteenth century, Spain was the dominant power in Middle America. The devastation of the great Indian civilizations was not only a result of military conquest but also of disease; European diseases were catastrophic to American Indians because their isolation had not allowed them to develop immunity to such common Old World illnesses as measles, influenza, and smallpox. The Spaniards replaced the Indian system of agriculture with livestock ranching, and the Indians of Middle America almost disappeared as an independent force.

III. The New World of Sixteenth-Century England

A. *Prices and Population*

The Spanish king used the fortune obtained in the New World in an attempt to expand his power throughout Europe. In the process he exhausted the resources of his state and left Spain in a process of decline. The lead in expanding European fortunes fell to France, Holland, and England. The intrusion of Spanish gold into European markets led to severe inflation. The need for money caused the English aristocracy to undergo a drastic reorganization. There was an increase in land ownership as prosperous tenants became landed gentry. The "price revolution" also brought about the enclosure movement, in which peasants found themselves barred from the use of formerly common grazing land. Forced out of agriculture, these landless peasants often migrated to the New World as indentured servants.

B. *Mercantilism and Colonization*

As the use of money became more widespread, merchants and bankers began to play a more important role in the English economy. The "putting out" system of manufacturing created a network of business enterprise. The Crown helped develop an economic system called mercantilism, which assisted the merchants while expanding the power and wealth of the nation. As a part of this royal enterprise, the English sought to challenge Spanish power in the New World. After several failed attempts, the English managed to found a permanent colony at Jamestown. The success of this settlement owed much to the development of the joint-stock company, a form of business organization that was able to provide sufficient funding for colonization.

C. Protestants and Puritans

The Protestant Reformation split the Roman Catholic world asunder. Although the different Protestant movements that emerged differed from each other in important ways, they were united in their opposition to the power, both spiritual and temporal, of the papacy. The Bible was translated into the language of the people of the various European nations, and the role of the laity was expanded. The Reformation in England was the least radical of the new movements. King replaced pope, the Bible was rendered into English, but little else changed at first. As the sixteenth century progressed, some English Protestants fell under the spell of Calvinism and began to demand more radical changes both in belief and in style. These Puritans, so-called because of their desire to purify the church, were in conflict with the Crown over the authority of the rulers in spiritual affairs. In the 1630s, the Archbishop of Canterbury initiated a severe persecution of Puritan clergymen and their congregations. Thousands of Puritans emigrated to the New World, while those remaining in England began to prepare for civil war.

ESSAY QUESTIONS

1. Describe the world of the preindustrial European peasants. How did they live? What work did they do? How were they affected by geography and climate?
2. How did the Roman Catholic church attempt to bring order to the lives of people in preindustrial Europe?
3. Describe the hierarchical structure of preindustrial Europe. In what ways did the structure of society resemble the structure of family life?
4. How did the relationship between war and trade alter the world view of Renaissance Europe?
5. Discuss the culture of the Aztecs at the time the Europeans arrived. What factors enabled the *conquistadors* to overcome the New World Indians?
6. In what ways did the "price revolution" alter the traditional structure of English society? How did these changes affect migration to the New World?
7. Discuss the rise of mercantilism, and indicate its impact on colonization and settlement in the New World.

8. In what ways did the emergence of the Protestant Reformation alter the religious world view of preindustrial Europe?
9. Discuss the rise of Puritanism within the Anglican tradition. What developments led Puritans to migrate in large numbers to the New World?
10. Compare and contrast the commercial and religious motivations of Europeans for discovery, conquest, and settlement in the New World.

IDENTIFICATIONS

Lady Day
Unam Sanctam
"infidels"
Leviathan
patriarchy
Crusades
Renaissance
Prince Henry the Navigator

Amerigo Vespucci
Tenochtitlán
Francisco Pizarro
yeoman farmer
enclosure movement
putting-out system
Presbyterianism
divine right of kings

PRIMARY SOURCE ANALYSIS

"Cambridge, Massachusetts, Platform for Admission into the Church" (p. 29)
1. How did the process for admission into the church at Cambridge differ from traditional Roman Catholic practice?
2. Who is to determine whether a candidate for church membership is acceptable?
3. What does the platform say are the dangers of standards for admission that are too low? What does the platform say are the dangers of standards of admission that are too high?

MAP EXERCISE

"The Expansion of Renaissance Europe" (p. 13)
1. How can this map help us to understand the religious significance of the discovery of certain new trade routes?
2. How can this map help to explain the relative decline of Italian trading cities during the Renaissance?
3. What trade goods did Columbus hope to acquire from his voyages?

ILLUSTRATION ANALYSIS

"A Dutch Merchant Family" (p. 15)
1. What aspects of this painting might reflect a religious sensibility?
2. Name the different foods that you can identify. What does the variety of foods suggest about the economic status of the family in the painting? Is anything missing from the table that you might expect to find at a feast?
3. What does this painting suggest about the attitude toward children in this period?

CHAPTER CONTEXT

This chapter describes the European world at the time of the discovery and initial colonization of the New World. The traditional agricultural society of Europe was undergoing rapid changes in patterns of belief and economic organization. The Renaissance and Reformation shattered the rigidly hierarchical structure of medieval life and began to provide new paths to social mobility. English society was seriously disrupted by a changing economic system and religious conflict. English colonists in the New World brought with them both the ideas of the new commercial world and the traditional desire for a unified, hierarchical society.

The next chapter will describe the attempts of European colonists to bring the New World under their political and cultural control.

2

A Century of Conflict, 1600–1700

OUTLINE AND SUMMARY

I. The Invasion of North America

A. *The Native Americans*

The 5–7 million Indians who lived in North America when the Europeans arrived lived in hundreds of small tribes. In the north, they tended to subsist on hunting and gathering, but farther south they had developed systems of agriculture. Highly devéloped civilizations had emerged in the Mississippi Valley under the influence of migrants from Middle America. These cultures established a comfortable agricultural civilization that had been in place for generations when the Europeans encountered them.

B. *European-Indian Interaction*

The three purposes of the European invasion of North America—religious, commercial, and imperialist—often determined the attitude different foreigners adopted toward the Indians. The Spanish missionaries in the Southwest vigorously sought to make Catholics out of the Native Americans. French missionary work, on the other hand, was less coercive; the Jesuits lived among the Indians and tried to work out an amalgamation of Catholic and Indian beliefs. Because the French were actively engaged in the fur trade, they needed the cooperation of the Indian tribes and therefore fostered friendly relations. The Dutch began their operations in North America with an eye to commerce but later came into conflict with the Indians as they sought to expand their agricultural holdings into Indian territory in what is now upstate New York. Almost from the beginning, the English intent to expand their initial settlements led inexorably to warfare with established Indian tribes.

C. The Conquest of New England

In New England the Puritans used their religion to justify the dispossession of the Indians. They argued that if God did not want it to happen, it would not happen. Following Old Testament precedent, the Puritans felt justified in waging war on the pagan Indians. The Indians fought back, of course, and brutal warfare broke out. The Puritans adopted the position that only by killing the Indians or driving them out of the territory could Puritan control of the Northeast be assured, and a genocidal struggle ensued.

D. The Indian Decline in the East

As a result of the warfare in New England and Virginia, the Indian tribes of the East Coast virtually disappeared. Captive Indians were enslaved and shipped to the Carolinas. Tribes in the interior found their traditional ways altered through trade with Europeans. The introduction of alcohol and iron had a major impact on Indian culture, and the pressure of the fur trade destroyed the traditional Indian relationship with nature. In adopting European technology and attitudes, the Indians underwent a period of rapid social change that saw the disappearance of many of their distinctive cultural traits.

II. Social Conflict in the Chesapeake Colonies

A. Tobacco and Disease

The Virginia Company offered land to English settlers in an attempt to encourage migration, and it indicated that American colonists would retain the rights of Englishmen. Among other things, this meant that landowners would play a part in the political system, and patterns of limited self-government began to appear in both Virginia and Maryland. The emergence of tobacco as a valuable crop in the Chesapeake colonies led to a sharp increase in migration to the area. The new population was beset with disease, however, with malaria leading to an extremely high death rate. Nevertheless, the promise of profit from tobacco kept the immigrants coming, as thousands sought their fortunes in tobacco and land. Along with the potential landowners came thousands of indentured servants, most of them young men from England's rootless poor.

B. *Economic Power and Political Privilege*

Much of the labor in the Chesapeake area was performed by indentured servants. Poor people in England sold themselves into temporary servitude in exchange for transportation to and subsistence in North America. Their lives were under the total control of their masters until they served out their indenture—typically four or five years. While life as a servant was particularly hard on young women, once they became free they had a good chance to marry well because of the drastic shortage of women in the area. When tobacco prices fell, the freed servants had difficulty managing their land grants and often sold the property to large landowners and worked as farm laborers. Wealthy planters increasingly dominated the Chesapeake region. Political corruption during the tenure in office of Governor William Berkeley and the growing number of landless poor in Virginia created a volatile situation.

C. *Bacon's Rebellion*

As the poorer farmers moved westward in Virginia, they sought the assistance of the political authorities in eliminating Indian resistance. Berkeley opposed the anti-Indian campaign and in turn was opposed by frontiersmen organized by Nathaniel Bacon, one of the few wealthy landowners with extensive holdings on the frontier. In the struggle for control of the colony, Bacon and his private army seized power and declared a war of extermination against the Indians. A civil war broke out between the Bacon and Berkeley forces. When the death of Bacon left his supporters in disarray, Berkeley resumed control of the colony. In order to prevent the conflict from recurring and to avert the further growth of a class of poor, landless whites, African slaves became the bound labor of choice.

III. Puritan New England

A. *The Puritan Covenant*

The Puritans of Massachusetts Bay saw themselves as central figures in God's plan for humankind. They would show the world how a Christian society should operate. They organized a political system that provided a representative government for the colony, with church members holding the franchise. The officials were to rule according to God's law. Puritan rejection of papal and episcopal authority led them to favor a congregational form of religious authority, with the laity playing a prominent role in church government. The Calvinist theology followed by the New England churches put great stress on the sinfulness of humankind and the doctrines of predestination and election. The believers were to remain always in doubt about their eternal security. The emergence of Arminian religious beliefs began to soften the harshness of strict Calvinism.

B. *The Suppression of Dissent*

Although the Puritans had developed a radical critique of former Christian belief and practice, they were not tolerant of further religious experimentation. They were strongly opposed to emerging notions of separation of church and state found in the Plymouth colony and in the teachings of Roger Williams. More threatening yet were the "antinomian" beliefs of Anne Hutchinson. Hutchinson offended the Puritan hierarchy both by her disregard for the traditional patriarchal view that women should not play a public role in religious affairs and in her teachings that individuals could and should have direct personal relations with God. Both Williams and Hutchinson were banished from Massachusetts Bay Colony and moved to Rhode Island. As time passed and religious fervor diminished, the Puritans had to make adjustments in their policies regarding church membership and political participation in order to maintain control of the colony.

C. *A Freeholding Society*

The Puritans believed that the goals of the "holy commonwealth" could best be achieved by a society of landowning families organized into a network of independent townships. To this end, land was granted to organized communities who distributed the land among themselves and ran their affairs through town meetings. The township chose representatives for the colony-wide government. There remained wide disparity between the extremes of wealth and poverty, but the economic base of the colony was the individual farm-owning family. Unlike the Chesapeake colonies, New England was not dominated by an aristocracy made up of the owners of large estates. Thus two contrasting cultural styles existed in the settlements of English North America in the seventeenth century.

ESSAY QUESTIONS

1. Compare and contrast the relationship between the Indians and colonists from Spain, France, and England. What factors contributed to the different patterns of Indian-white relations that emerged?
2. On what basis did the Puritans justify their policy toward the Indians? What were the results of that policy?

3. How was Indian culture affected by the contact with Europeans in the seventeenth century?
4. How did tobacco and disease contribute to the development of the Chesapeake colonies?
5. What role did indentured servitude play in the Chesapeake colonies? What happened to the immigrants, male and female, when they had served out their indentures?
6. What factors led to Bacon's Rebellion in Virginia? How was this struggle resolved?
7. What religious principles influenced the organization of Massachusetts Bay Colony? How were these principles translated into political organization?
8. Discuss the religious views of Roger Williams and Anne Hutchinson. Describe and evaluate the official Puritan response to these dissenters.
9. Discuss and evaluate the process through which Massachusetts Bay Colony organized itself economically and politically as a society of freeholders.
10. Compare and contrast the political and economic structures of the Chesapeake colonies and New England.

IDENTIFICATIONS

Natchez Indians
coureurs de bois
Opechancanough
Pequot Indians
John Eliot
King Philip's War
House of Burgesses
indenture

Acts of Trade and Navigation
Nathaniel Bacon
Congregationalists
"millennialists"
Roger Williams
Halfway Covenant
Cambridge Platform of 1648
freeholder

PRIMARY SOURCE ANALYSIS

"The Puritan Vision of an Ideal Society" (p. 55)
1. Why does Winthrop believe that Massachusetts Bay Colony should be a "city upon a hill"?
2. What is Hutchinson accused of? Why was this a problem?
3. How does Hutchinson defend herself? What do you think she means by "some public times"?

MAP EXERCISE

"Settlement Patterns in New England" (p. 58)
1. What do you think the blue lines on the map of Wethersfield represent?
2. In which town—Andover or Wethersfield—do you think the terrain is more level? Why? Could this have affected the decision for "nucleated" or "dispersed" settlement patterns?
3. What reasons other than those mentioned in the caption can you think of for the maintenance of nucleated villages in the Connecticut River valley?

ILLUSTRATION ANALYSIS

"The Indian Village of Pomeiock" (p. 40)
1. How were Indian beds constructed? Why?
2. What does the Indian housing suggest about the class structure within the tribe?
3. Were fires built inside the houses? How can you tell? What do you think were the purposes of the large central fire?

CHAPTER CONTEXT

The previous chapter described the culture of preindustrial Europe and indicated forces leading to the conquest and settlement of the New World.

This chapter introduces the New World explorations of the Spanish and French and goes on to describe in some detail the early settlements of the English. Focusing on two regions—the Chesapeake colonies (Virginia and Maryland) and New England—the chapter presents the motivations for settlement and development in those areas. The Indian population was suppressed or driven out, and contrasting systems of agriculture and land tenure emerged. The Chesapeake colonies were dominated by wealthy owners of large estates, while individual freeholding farm families were more common in New England. By the end of the seventeenth century, the English coastal settlements in both regions were secure from Indian attack and were expanding into the interior.

The next chapter will explore the emergence of a distinctly American culture in the colonial settlements.

3

The Creation of an American Political System and Economy

OUTLINE AND SUMMARY

I. The Transformation of American Politics

A. The New Mercantilism

In order to strengthen mercantilism, the English government began to stress the regulation of colonial trade. Various Acts of Trade and Navigation gave the English merchant marine a monopoly on colonial trade and required that goods destined for the Continent be shipped through England. New colonies in North America were founded by the Crown—proprietary colonies, which were granted to prominent individuals in an effort to exercise closer control over colonial development. In practice, however, the proprietors were able to avoid royal authority. King James II established the Dominion of New England in 1685 as a way of asserting control over formerly self-governing colonies in that area.

B. The Glorious Revolution

Opposition to the religious and commercial policies of James II led Parliament to replace him with his daughter and son-in-law, Mary II and William of Orange, in 1688. This "Glorious Revolution" contributed to the breakup of the Dominion of New England and to emerging opposition in other colonies to the colonial policies of the English government. Although the mercantile policies remained in force, the restoration of a measure of self-government in the colonies enabled Americans to continue to develop their own institutional life.

C. Society and Politics

In the seventeenth century, elites dominated colonial political life. Even where there were representative assemblies, the operant political philosophy caused power to flow down from the top. Then, as the Glorious Revolution began to shift the power of government in England toward Parliament, authority in the colonies began to shift toward the representative assemblies. An important factor in the development of a more democratic system was the growth of kin networks in the colonies. Certain families tended to dominate political life in individual communities. As the suffrage spread, the voters tended to maintain the colonial elite in office. But the governing officials could not ignore the will of the common people because they did not have the power to enforce policies that the community did not support.

D. "Salutary Neglect"

During the first half of the eighteenth century, the British relaxed their control of colonial affairs. This policy of "salutary neglect" left the colonies to develop their institutional life relatively free of British intrusion. The political struggles in England between the followers of Sir Robert Walpole and the Real Whigs also had a significant effect on colonial life. During this period, most of the Crown representatives placed in positions of authority in the Americas were of mediocre quality, giving the colonial assemblies an opportunity to enhance their power. By midcentury, the assemblies were actually in charge of their own affairs, a control they secured by establishing for themselves the right to levy all the taxes necessary for colonial administration.

II. The South Atlantic Slave Economy

A. The South Atlantic System

British power in the early eighteenth century was built on the colonial economy of the South Atlantic. The basic crop of the area was sugar, grown with the use of African slave labor in the West Indies. Since most of the owners of the sugar plantations lived in England, the high profits from their operations went directly into the British economy. This process had a negative effect on West Africa, however. The slave trade drained millions of young people from West Africa and led to a political and economic transformation of the regions that supplied the slaves for the trade. Where there had been loosely organized tribal federations, there arose tightly knit political structures that maintained powerful military units who waged war to supply captives for the slave trade. In this process, both the moral tone and economic potential of West Africa suffered.

B. Virginia's Decision for Slavery

Initially, the British colonies in North America did not practice chattel slavery; the first Africans in Virginia probably became free people. The early English migrants to the New World had a strong belief in individual liberty. Soon, however, the African laborers were being treated differently from the white servants. The fact that the Africans were pagans, not Christians, contributed to the increasing differentiation between black and white bound labor. By the 1660s, laws in the Chesapeake colonies were distinguishing blacks from whites in cases dealing with bound labor. The late seventeenth century saw the emergence of legal chattel slavery of Africans in English North America.

C. The Slave Economy

For slaves imported into the sugar economy of the Caribbean, life was brutal and short. The policy of the plantation managers was to work a slave to death and replace him with another. In the North American colonies, on the other hand, the physical labor required of the slaves was less demanding. As a result, slaves lived longer. An increase in the number of female slaves in the Chesapeake region made it possible for the slaves to increase their number through natural reproduction. The slaveowners began to realize that encouraging the slaves to breed would increase their own capital holdings. In the eighteenth century, the Chesapeake colonies began to replace their white labor with black, and the slave economy was firmly established. Farther south, African labor and agricultural expertise were used to develop a thriving rice economy in the lowlands of South Carolina, and the profits from this enterprise elevated the plantation owners to power there. By the time of the War of American Independence, slaves made up a fifth of the population of the North American colonies, and their presence had a significant impact on the moral quality of American life for blacks and whites alike.

D. The Northern Commercial Economy

Although there were few African slaves in the northern colonies, the merchants and farmers of the area became deeply involved in the South Atlantic System. New England and the Middle Atlantic colonies provided food for the sugar islands. The islands in turn shipped molasses to New England, where it was distilled into rum, which was used to barter for slaves in West Africa. The trade with the Caribbean also provided money for use in the American domestic economy. American merchants developed a near-monopoly on trade with the West Indies, and British commercial interests persuaded Parliament to put controls on American trade by passing the Molasses Act of 1732. This restriction, never rigidly enforced, was the beginning of a fateful struggle between the colonies and the mother country over trade policy. A conflict over monetary policy also arose as colonial bankers began to issue paper money on the strength of land holdings. Parliament tried to end this policy by passing the Currency Acts of 1751 and 1764. As colonial autonomy increased, certain officials in England began to question the continuation of the policy of salutary neglect.

ESSAY QUESTIONS

1. How did the mercantile policies of the British government in the second half of the seventeenth century affect the North American colonies?
2. What impact did the Glorious Revolution have on the political structure of the colonies?
3. What is meant by the policy of "salutary neglect"? How did this policy affect colonial development?
4. Discuss and evaluate the factors that led to the increase in the power of colonial assemblies in the seventeenth and early eighteenth centuries.
5. Describe the structure of the South Atlantic System. What elements of the system contributed to the development of African slavery?
6. Discuss and evaluate the factors that led the Chesapeake colonies to adopt the legal system of chattel slavery.
7. Compare and contrast the agricultural technology of the American Indians and the Africans as it affected the development of colonial America.
8. Discuss and evaluate the role played by African slaves in the development of American agriculture in the seventeenth and early eighteenth centuries.
9. How did the northern colonies become involved in the South Atlantic System? What impact did this development have on British mercantilism?
10. Discuss and evaluate the conflict in the seventeenth and early eighteenth centuries between the colonial assemblies and the authorities set over them by the British government.

IDENTIFICATIONS

proprietary colony
Dominion of New England
Sir Edmund Andros
Glorious Revolution

"middle passage"
Acts of Trade and Navigation
Jacob Leisler
chattel slavery

Whig party
"salutary neglect"
Board of Trade
Sir Robert Walpole

South Atlantic System
Molasses Act
land bank
Currency Act

PRIMARY SOURCE ANALYSIS

"The Brutal 'Middle Passage,' 1735" (p. 77)
1. What might Equiano have meant by referring to his "former slavery"?
2. Why was Equiano forcibly fed?
3. Why do you suppose the Africans tried to jump overboard?

MAP EXERCISE

"The Rise of the American Merchant" (p. 85)
1. How does this map demonstrate the advantages that American merchants enjoyed over the British in the trade depicted here?
2. Where did the rum used in the slave trade originate?
3. Why did the American colonies export rice and fish to the Mediterranean rather than to England? Would Britain have tried to restrict this trade? Why?

ILLUSTRATION ANALYSIS

"Passage on a Slave Ship" (p. 78)
1. About how many slaves could be crowded onto the lower deck of the slave ship depicted in the diagram?
2. Compare the apparent density of the slave "cargo" shown in the two illustrations.
3. Do you think the Africans shown in the watercolor are from one tribal or language group or from a mixture? Why?

CHAPTER CONTEXT

The previous chapter described the first settlements of English North America in the seventeenth century.

The present chapter explores the developments in the British colonies in the New World between 1650 and 1750. Reflecting the changes in British politics during this period, the colonies saw the rise of the representative assembly as the basis of American political life. Although the legal structure of mercantilism remained intact, the Americans were allowed a fairly free rein in developing their own commercial policies. The adoption of African slavery in North America enabled the colonies to produce staple crops and a surplus of foodstuffs that could be sold to the sugar islands, bringing profit to American farmers and merchants. The policy of "salutary neglect" began to be challenged at the end of the period, as Americans became more independent and self-sufficient.

The next chapter will look at the emergence of distinct regional cultures in British North America before 1750.

4

The Cultures of Preindustrial America

OUTLINE AND SUMMARY

I. Northern Freehold Society

A. The Lineal Farm Family

The possibility of land ownership was one of the main reasons people migrated to America, and, in the northern colonies, 70 percent of the land was controlled by freeholding farm families. Farm owners had to be concerned not only with themselves, but also with their descendants. If a father did not own sufficient land to pass along to his children, they were doomed to start adult life as laborers. Several devices were adopted to provide for children of landowners. Among them were the "entail" and "stem family" systems, which passed the land along intact to one son while providing for other heirs in different ways. Fathers who tried to divide their estates among their children saw the holdings become too small to operate successfully. Careful marshaling of resources, as well as inheritance patterns, enabled the northern colonies to maintain a freeholding society for generations.

B. Women's Place

As was the case in Europe, women played a subordinate role in the colonies. Religious teachings and cultural tradition insisted that women were to serve as obedient daughters and subservient wives. When she married, a woman's property was bestowed on her husband, and she remained totally dependent on him for subsistence. Since most colonial families were agricultural, women performed a variety of processing tasks associated with farm life—spinning, weaving, and preserving food, for example. Women married in their early twenties and spent the next twenty years bearing and rearing children. The women in German, French-Canadian, and Scotch-Irish communities regularly worked in the fields alongside their men, while Puritan wives rarely did so.

C. Malthus and America

The Malthusian crisis of population outstripping food supply was averted in the American colonies by agricultural innovation and westward migration. In New England, younger sons increasingly moved to frontier areas as the amount of available land at home diminished. Farmers in the region began to plant rye, apple orchards, corn, and potatoes in an effort to maintain a healthful food supply both for themselves and for their livestock. The close-knit kin networks in New England created cooperative enterprise and an effective barter system. The middle colonies, with their rich soil and longer growing season, raised wheat for export and grew prosperous in the process. The profits from trade began to create class differentiation in Pennsylvania, as it became more difficult for newer immigrants to obtain satisfactory farmland. The middle colonies began to see the rise of a class of landless farm laborers, in spite of attempts by the proprietors to maintain a freeholding society. In New York, the longstanding semifeudal system discouraged immigration until landlords made tenant farming more attractive in the estate areas. As colonial society became more complex and economically differentiated, small freeholders saw their position become more marginal, and they turned to political activity in an attempt to make their future more secure.

II. Masters and Slaves

A. The Traditional Social Order Restored

In the seventeenth century, life in the Chesapeake colonies was difficult. Disease and death prevented the creation of a stable kin-linked community like that in New England. The shortage of women gave the women who survived a more important role in family legal affairs than would otherwise have been the case. By the mid-eighteenth century, however, society in the region had been stabilized and the traditional social order had been restored. A major factor in this development was the rise of slave labor on the agricultural plantations in the area. The wealthy landowners who dominated Virginia society granted political power to the small farmers of the region in an attempt to hold their support. In this way, the slaveowning elite in the Chesapeake colonies achieved the status of a stable ruling class.

B. *Oppression and Resistance*

The wealthy elite of the southern colonies built their power on the back of slave labor. The forms of control exercised over the slave population were brutal and violent. In the eighteenth century, slavery increasingly became a system of total control over the lives of the slaves. The enslaved Africans sought to oppose the system by a variety of techniques. They deliberately worked slowly and incompetently, they stole from their masters, and, in extreme cases, they engaged in violent resistance. When slaves rebelled, as they did in New York City and South Carolina, the violent repression that resulted tended to discourage this form of activity. But resentment smoldered among the slave population, and thousands of blacks fled to the British camp when the War of American Independence broke out.

C. *The Creation of an Afro-American Society*

The blacks enslaved in the New World came from a variety of tribal backgrounds; their specific tribal identity was stronger for them than their African origin. Over time, however, they tended to adopt the English language or a general dialect like Gullah. After a generation or two in America, an Afro-American culture began to emerge. Unlike in other New World slaveholding societies, American culture made no place for those of mixed racial ancestry; in the British colonies, a person was either white or black. Afro-American culture derived from attempts by the slaves to build a community based on memory, kinship, and religion. Drawing on their African past, their present living conditions, and their hopes for the future, slaves constructed an existence for themselves outside the control of their masters.

III. Toward a New Social Order

A. *Ethnic Diversity*

The religious freedom and rich land of the Middle Colonies (especially Pennsylvania) attracted immigrants from a variety of European countries. Religious discrimination and worsening economic conditions led to the migration of 150,000 Scotch-Irish, most of whom arrived in Philadelphia and settled in the back country of Pennsylvania and the Carolinas. Another major source of middle-colony immigrants was Germany. Persecuted religious minorities were welcomed by William Penn, and in later generations Pennsylvania remained a haven for dissident religious groups. Other Germans, often whole families, came as redemptioners, a form of indentured servant. More prosperous Germans settled in what came to be called the Pennsylvania Dutch country in the eastern part of the colony and engaged in the profitable wheat trade. The new immigrants tended to keep their ethnic ties intact, and, in the case of the Germans, language was a particularly cohesive factor.

B. Quakers and Political Pluralism

Although strong ethnic prejudice existed in New England and to a certain extent in New York, the Quaker heritage in Pennsylvania led to religious toleration there. The Quakers were the most radical of the Reformation movements to settle in large numbers in North America. In sharp contrast to the Puritans, they believed that all people were able to achieve salvation and that, since God could speak through any man or woman, there was no need for a trained clergy. Quakers refused to cooperate with many aspects of governmental authority and rejected the notion of a social hierarchy. In Pennsylvania, the pacifism of the Quakers led them to avoid violent conflict with the Indians. Although the Quakers did not use governmental authority to enforce religious practices, they applied stringent community pressure to establish conformity among themselves. One outcome of that procedure was the formation of a powerful and coherent landowning class of Quakers, which dominated Pennsylvania affairs. Non-Quaker religious communities on the frontier united in political opposition to the eastern-based Quakers.

C. Regional Provincialism

By the mid-eighteenth century, many families in the British colonies had been in America for several generations. Throughout the New World, separation from their homelands had weakened colonists' national cultural ties, but these had not yet been replaced with a distinctly American identity. British North America was made up of regional cultures that reflected different national origins. The English immigrants built houses in the English style, and the Germans copied their nation's distinctive architecture. Most houses in all regions were small, consisting of only one or two rooms. Crowded conditions prevailed in the New World, as they had in the Old, and privacy was unknown. As wealth increased in the colonies, however, the elite began to build larger houses and to import items for household use. In this process, they adopted patterns of English culture, which began to drive a wedge between themselves and the mass of the population. At the same time, however, the English overlay began to provide some cultural unity to the diverse regions of North America.

ESSAY QUESTIONS

1. What patterns of inheritance were adopted in New England to ensure the continuance of a freeholding society?
2. What was the legal position of women in northern colonial society? What role did women play in the domestic economy?
3. How did colonial agriculture adapt to avoid the Malthusian crisis?
4. Discuss and evaluate the factors that contributed to the growth of class distinctions in the middle colonies.
5. Discuss the process through which a stable ruling class emerged in the Chesapeake colonies.
6. Discuss and evaluate the different ways in which the slaves resisted the oppressive slave system.
7. Describe the process through which Africans became Afro-Americans.
8. Compare and contrast the major ethnic groups who settled in the middle colonies in the early eighteenth century.
9. Analyze the aspects of Quakerism that had a significant impact on the development of Pennsylvania.
10. Compare and contrast the regional cultures that dominated colonial life in the early eighteenth century.

IDENTIFICATIONS

"stem family"
entail
"dower rights"
Thomas Malthus
"inmates"
Scotch-Irish
Stono uprising
Gullah

miscegenation
Pennsylvania Dutch
Gottlieb Mittelburger
Society of Friends
Georgian architecture
cultural pluralism
William Penn
"redemptioners"

PRIMARY SOURCE ANALYSIS

"William Penn's Charter of Privileges, 1701" (p. 109)
1. What are the religious qualifications for the holding of political office in Pennsylvania?

2. Does this charter uphold the right of rebellion against the government? Explain your answer.
3. What would be the place of members of the Jewish religion in Pennsylvania?

MAP EXERCISE

"Ethnic Diversity" (p. 106)
1. Compare this map with the one on page 103. Which non-English ethnic group was most likely to keep slaves?
2. Trace on the map the path of the Scotch-Irish migration from Philadelphia to the Shenandoah Valley. What other major ethnic group settled in that valley?
3. Locate the Pennsylvania Dutch country on the map.

ILLUSTRATION ANALYSIS

"Self-Portrait of an Artist at Work" (p. 94)
1. Which items in the picture did the needlework artist probably make?
2. What does the caption writer mean by the comment that the picture contains symbols of the artist's mortality?
3. What elements in the picture help us determine the social class of the artist?

CHAPTER CONTEXT

The last chapter described the changing economic and political systems in the American colonies.

This chapter explores the developing regional cultures in America. The northern colonies maintained a freeholding society by carefully watching inheritance patterns and adapting their agricultural practices where necessary. The middle colonies saw an enormous influx of migration, particularly Scotch-Irish and Germans who were attracted by Pennsylvania's religious toleration. Southern culture was influenced by the widespread adoption of African slavery. While Africans were developing cultural forms that could support them against their oppression, the southern elite kept itself in power by granting extended political privileges to the less wealthy whites in the region. The growing prosperity of the colonies was not equally shared but led to an increasing economic disparity between the classes, with the wealthy turning toward England as a source of high culture.

The next chapter will see England playing an increasingly critical role in America as colonial life expands and becomes more complex.

5

The Convergence of Europe and America

OUTLINE AND SUMMARY

I. The Enlightenment and Pietistic Religion

A. Magic and Science

The world of colonial America was filled with supernatural occurrences. For the devout, God often worked in miraculous ways. But when otherwise ordinary men and women seemed to have access to miraculous power, they were often accused of being wizards or witches and were punished. Opposing the emphasis on the supernatural, Enlightenment thinking focused on the use of human reason to understand the mysteries of the created order. The scientific theories of Isaac Newton and the philosophy of John Locke began to point the way to the use of scientific method to achieve knowledge. Enlightenment humanism predicted an improved world through the application of human effort. This kind of thinking was widespread among the elite and influenced the founding of educational institutions. Deists saw no conflict between the emerging science and their religious beliefs.

B. Pietism

Pietism emerged in Europe as a way of establishing an emotional tie between man and God. Brought to the colonies first from Germany and later by John Wesley and George Whitefield, pietism used emotional preaching and prayer meetings to "wake up" the souls of men to the threat of eternal damnation. The Great Awakening of the mid-eighteenth century had a permanent impact on American religious life.

Many traditional churches and denominations split over the issues raised by the methodology of the Great Awakening. Pietist preachers and congregations broke away from the traditions of a formal institutional structure and an educated clergy, leading to an increase in Baptist churches. Pietist leaders were also able to break the monopoly of the legally established churches in New England, while, on the frontier, pietism helped strengthen the communal values of agricultural life. Those religious leaders influenced by Enlightenment thought tended to put an emphasis on individual effort and pursuit of the good life for self and society. A fateful conflict between these two religious movements began to emerge.

C. Conflict in Virginia

In Virginia, the legally established Church of England held the loyalty of the upper classes, who controlled the churches through the vestry system. The clergymen who filled Anglican pulpits in Virginia were of mediocre quality and remained under the thumb of the gentry. The message of the Great Awakening appealed to the poorer settlers on the frontier, where the New Lights and Baptists were organizing congregations, contrary to the laws of the colony. Law-enforcement authorities persecuted the nonestablishment clergy in an attempt to prevent the spread of pietistic Protestantism. The "awakened" Christians were critical of what they saw as the immoral way of life of the Anglican gentry, and they continued to form pietist churches. The conflict between Anglicans and the new churches reflected a growing class antagonism in the Chesapeake region. The pietists were not political activists, however, and the control of the colony remained in the hands of the planter elite.

II. Economic Expansion and Social Structure

A. Transatlantic Trade

The Industrial Revolution in Great Britain made more manufactured products available for sale in the colonies. At the same time, the increase of the colonial population spurred demand for those products. The result was a sharp increase in transatlantic trade. In order to pay for the trade, American colonists stepped up their production of commodities for export—particularly tobacco, indigo, and wheat. Also important in the transatlantic trade were items of American manufacture. Rum and refined sugar were exported from New England. The forests provided lumber for shipbuilding and other construction uses. Colonial-built ships began to dominate the British merchant marine. In the process of developing domestic manufacturing, the colonies took a major step toward self-sufficiency.

B. Urban Growth and Social Diversity

Increasing trade brought with it urban growth and a more complex division of labor in the colonies. The port cities of the eastern seaboard—Boston, Newport, New York, Philadelphia, Baltimore, and Charleston—each experienced dramatic growth in the eighteenth century. The labor requirements of expanding commerce drew many workers to the enterprise. Much of the heavy labor of the ports was done by slaves, indentured servants, or poor whites who barely managed to eke out an existence. The demands of internal trade caused the rise of small towns and villages in the back country, which served as commercial centers for the export of agricultural products and the distribution of manufactured goods. A large number of artisans were necessary to produce and maintain the means of transportation—wagons, barrels, crates, and so on. The colonial economy continued to be dominated by a small, wealthy elite whose fortunes were based on commerce. As real estate values and food costs rose in the cities, free white laborers found themselves in a precarious economic position. The reliance on commerce caused economic cycles that regularly threatened the livelihoods of those engaged in trade, and also contributed to the growing awareness of class distinctions in colonial society.

III. The Struggle for the American Land

A. Who Owns the Land?

As the good farmland in New England and the middle colonies began to fill up, disputes arose over land ownership and proprietary rights. Farm families began to move into areas where borders were disputed and the question of land title obscure. Tenants rebelled, seeking ownership of land held on long-term leases. Colonial authorities suppressed these rebellions and reasserted the terms of the original colonial charters. Proprietors ousted squatters from long-held lands in the interest of increasing their income from rent and land sales. Inexpensive land became harder to obtain, and the increasingly powerful colonial governments were able to restore or maintain the quasi-feudal nature of the original grants. Landless tenants and small yeoman farm families found themselves in an increasingly marginal economic position.

B. The Great War for Empire

As the settlers in New York moved ever westward, they began to come into conflict with the Iroquois Indians and the French. The Indians managed to preserve their territory by playing the colonial powers against each other. But migration of English colonists into the Ohio

Valley led to war between the English and the French. Although the much greater numbers of English settlers almost guaranteed a British victory, the war progressed slowly because of the wilderness conditions. Their victory in America assured, the British used their maritime advantage to pursue their struggle against the French worldwide, and in the process established the basis for the mighty British Empire of the nineteenth century. Military policy led the British to establish firmer control over colonial affairs in America, a development that opened up further areas of conflict between the American colonies and the British government.

C. Western Settlers and Eastern Interests

Settlers on the frontier continued to challenge the authority of the colonial governments. A particular area of conflict had to do with Indian policy. Frontiersmen wanted to get rid of the Indians, while colonial authorities preferred peaceful relationships. Back-country settlers organized themselves into bands of raiders and took the law into their own hands. In Pennsylvania, the Paxton Boys massacred Indians and marched on Philadelphia. South Carolina Regulators tried to bring order to the outlaw-ridden western part of the colony. In North Carolina, Regulators organized in opposition to the financial pressures put on the frontier farmers. In all of these cases, colonial authorities were able to defeat the insurgent movements, but the conflicts left bitter memories and had a significant impact on the upcoming struggle for independence.

ESSAY QUESTIONS

1. In what ways did the emerging scientific world view of the colonial period challenge the beliefs of traditional religion?
2. Discuss and evaluate the impact of pietism on Protestantism in colonial America. What effect did this movement have on existing denominations?
3. Analyze religious conflict in Virginia as a reflection of social class struggle.
4. In what ways did the transatlantic trade of the eighteenth century contribute to the increased self-sufficiency of the colonies?
5. Analyze the class structure of colonial cities, indicating the economic and political factors that reinforced it.
6. What factors led to the reemergence of land ownership as a major issue in the colonies in the mid-eighteenth century? What was the outcome of this development?

7. Through what process did the French and Indian War become the Great War for Empire?
8. How did the French and Indian War lead to an increasing divergence of interests between the American colonies and Britain?
9. Describe the emergence of Regulator movements on the colonial frontier. What issues concerned them, and what were the results of their activities?
10. Discuss and evaluate the class struggle in the American colonies in the first two-thirds of the eighteenth century. What were the sources of conflict? How was the struggle carried on? How would you characterize the distribution of power throughout the period?

IDENTIFICATIONS

the "new learning"
John Locke
deism
jeremiad
George Whitefield
New Lights
Twopenny Acts
indigo

Iroquois
Ohio Company
Albany "Plan of Union"
Treaty of Paris (1763)
Pontiac
Paxton Boys
William Pitt
Regulators

PRIMARY SOURCE ANALYSIS

"Debate over Colonial Price Controls" (p. 141)
1. What is the "impudent combination" complained about in the first selection? Why do you think the writer uses the term "impudent"?
2. Who was fined for breaking the law?
3. What is the concept of "liberty" proposed by the proponents of price controls?

MAP EXERCISE

"European Spheres of Influence, 1754" (p. 145)
1. If you were a British strategic planner in 1754, where would this map lead you to expect the main campaigns in a war with France to occur?
2. Using the map on page 182, evaluate your own predictions. Were your answers to question 1 correct?

3. During the negotiations to end the Great War for Empire, what would you demand if you were British? What would you try to salvage if you were French?

ILLUSTRATION ANALYSIS

"The Architecture of Worship" (p. 134)
1. How many tiers are there in the pulpit of the Anglican church? Why?
2. What does the architecture of the two churches suggest about the two congregations' conceptions of the social order?
3. The caption states that "wooden barriers separated families from one another." Do you believe that this architectural feature had religious significance? Explain your answer.

CHAPTER CONTEXT

The previous chapter discussed the regional cultures emerging in colonial America.

This chapter describes how the increasing importance of the colonies led to a closer involvement with European affairs. New movements in science and religion began to take root in the colonies and contributed to a widening of social differences. American manufacturing and agricultural production increased sharply to meet the demands of the transatlantic trade. As the North American colonies began to grow stronger and more self-sufficient, the British government showed concern. The French and Indian War gave the British an opportunity to play a stronger role in colonial affairs, a development that many Americans resented. Social conflict within the colonies became widespread, as settlers on the frontier demanded a larger role in the determination of policy. The authority of the colonial governments was reasserted by force, but the social divisions remained a source of dissatisfaction.

The next chapter will explore the issues which led to the outbreak of the War of Independence.

6

Toward Independence: A Decade of Decisions

OUTLINE AND SUMMARY

I. Reform and Resistance

A. Background for Revolution

The cost of the French and Indian War led the British to reassert control over colonial trade. They sought to put an end to smuggling and corruption in the customs service. New legislation from Parliament sought to restrict colonial trade with non-British ports in the West Indies. In order to enforce the new edicts, the jurisdiction of the Vice-Admiralty Courts (nonjury trials) was extended. The growing power of the British government threatened the de facto freedom of the colonial assemblies, which attacked the new trade policies for having imposed taxation without representation. In reaction to colonial opposition, the British government assigned troops to keep the peace in America and enforce the Proclamation Line of 1763 barring migration west of the Appalachian Mountains.

B. The Stamp Act

In order to pay for the support of the British troops in America, Parliament proposed the Stamp Act for the colonies; this act could have been avoided had the colonies agreed to coordinate the raising of sufficient funds to pay the expenses of the troops. The colonial governments failed to do so, however, and Parliament passed the Stamp Act of 1765.

Violators of the act might face trial in the Vice-Admiralty Courts. The Quartering Act that followed required colonial legislatures to provide logistical support for British troops. Parliament had issued a significant challenge to colonial authority.

C. The Crowd Rebels
Although the British had expected resistance to the new measures, the intensity of the subsequent rioting astonished them. As a colonial Stamp Act Congress prepared to meet to coordinate resistance measures, crowds of city dwellers, known as Sons of Liberty, took matters in their own hands and violently attacked officials responsible for enforcing the Stamp Act. There was a previous tradition of disciplined mob action in both America and Britain, and colonists defended the Stamp Act riots as expressions of the popular will.

D. A Political Legacy
The Stamp Act Congress tried to find a compromise position between political rebellion and acquiescence. Arguing on the basis of the rights of trial by jury and taxation only by consent, the Congress petitioned Parliament to repeal the stamp tax. Violence broke out in the colonies wherever enforcement of the Stamp Act was attempted. Organized noncooperation with British policy was widely effective in port cities, and a sense of an American identity began to emerge. Even though most colonists continued to think of themselves as Englishmen, the authority of the mother country was fatefully undermined in the Stamp Act crisis.

II. The Growing Confrontation

A. The Constitutional Debate
British politics in the 1760s was confused because of a struggle for primacy between the Crown and Parliament. The king kept changing prime ministers, preventing a coherent colonial policy from emerging. The Rockingham administration followed a conciliatory path, repealing the Stamp Act and refusing to send more troops to suppress the rebellion in North America. Parliament continued to claim, however, that it had a right to dictate colonial policy. British politicians were divided over the nature of colonial representation in Parliament. Colonial authorities, on the other hand, were clear in their belief that North Americans had all the rights of British subjects, including the right of self-government. Therefore, they continued to resist Parliament's attempts to control colonial affairs.

B. The Townshend Duties

When the Rockingham faction collapsed, the task of formulating colonial policy fell to Charles Townshend, the Chancellor of the Exchequer. Determined that the colonies would pay for the troops stationed there, Townshend proposed a series of acts that would raise money through customs duties. Some of the money raised thereby was to pay the salaries of colonial officials, freeing them from the control of the local assemblies. American politicians and political bodies condemned the Townshend duties as unlawful and organized a successful nonimportation movement. The sharp decline in British trade led Parliament to repeal the duties, but the conflict over policy remained.

C. The Threat of Coercion

Struggle between the New York legislature and Parliament over support of British troops in North America led to the passage of the Restraining Act (1767), which gave Parliament the right to suspend colonial assemblies that refused to enforce its edicts. On the verge of applying military force to bring the colonies into line, the Crown began to adopt a more conciliatory posture. Under the ministry of Lord North, all import duties were abolished except the one on tea, which was kept for symbolic purposes. Although immediate conflict was averted, the colonists increasingly argued that their legislative bodies were on the same level as Parliament. It became clear that if Parliament were to achieve supremacy over the colonial assemblies, it would have to be through force.

III. Roots of Resistance

A. Urbanism and Ideology

The cities of colonial America provided the cauldron in which revolution was brewed. Urban merchants opposed British policies that interfered with the freedom of trade (and profit). Lawyers came to play prominent roles in political debate. Three intellectual traditions formed the basis of the colonial policy of resistance to British authority. The first was the right of trial by jury, enunciated in the Magna Carta and violated by the Vice-Admiralty Courts. The second was the Enlightenment notion of rationalism. The "natural rights" philosophy was to take the place of decision based on precedent. The third was the Whig tradition of resistance to autocratic power. The formulation of a political philosophy based on these three elements provided intellectual support for the emerging rebellion against British rule.

B. The Tea Act

Each conflict with British authority drew the colonists closer together. The tea crisis of 1773, in which the colonists violently resisted the establishment of a monopoly on tea for the British East Indian Company, exhausted the patience of Parliament. After the Boston Tea Party, the British government passed a series of "Intolerable Acts" to punish the port of Boston and the colony of Massachusetts. Shortly thereafter, the First Continental Congress met to formulate a response to the British policies. New England and the southern colonies were ready to commence military action, but the middle colonies sought a compromise structure that could preserve colonial rights and liberties within the British Empire. The compromise plan was defeated, and Congress declared financial war against the mother country. Parliament refused to budge, and the commander of the British forces in North America was ordered to quell the rebellion in Massachusetts.

C. The Rising of the Countryside

The colonial rebellion began in the cities but soon spread to the back country. The nonimportation policy reduced the level of consumer spending and received moral backing from the clergy and politicians. British military officials treated the colonists with contempt, arousing pride in an American identity. The rural settlements began to feel the economic pinch of British policy and felt their yeoman way of life threatened by Parliament's actions. Plantation owners seeking self-sufficiency sought to reduce their indebtedness to the British financial community by supporting nonimportation. In late 1774 the British army began to confiscate colonial armories and storehouses, leading the Continental Congress to raise an army of its own. Then, in April 1775, the British army marched on the colonial depot in Concord, Massachusetts, and in the process engaged in battle with colonial forces. The War of American Independence had begun.

ESSAY QUESTIONS

1. In what ways did the French and Indian War strain the resources of the British Empire? What steps did Parliament take to require the colonies to pay what it saw as their share of colonial expenses?
2. What did the colonists mean when they insisted that they should have all "the rights and privileges of Englishmen"? In what respects did Parliament's attitude on this matter differ from the colonists'?

3. Describe the provisions and the purposes of the Stamp Act. How did the colonists react to the application of the Stamp Act?
4. Discuss and evaluate the debate over colonial policy in Parliament during the 1760s.
5. Describe the provisions of the Townshend Acts, and evaluate the colonial reaction to their application.
6. In what ways and for what reasons was the rebellious attitude of the colonists transformed into a revolutionary movement? What were the intellectual underpinnings of this transformation?
7. What was the significance of the Boston Tea Party? Why was it organized, and what was its result?
8. Why was the First Continental Congress convened? What policies did it formulate prior to the outbreak of the War of Independence?
9. What economic factors played a role in the growing revolutionary attitude of the American colonists?
10. Discuss and evaluate the attempts of the British government to use military force to quell the colonial rebellion.

IDENTIFICATIONS

Vice-Admiralty Courts
George Grenville
Quartering Act
Sons of Liberty
Stamp Act Congress
King George III
Lord Rockingham
Townshend Acts

nonimportation
Restraining Act
John Adams
"Real Whigs"
Tea Act (1773)
"Coercive Acts"
Quebec Act
Committees of Correspondence

PRIMARY SOURCE ANALYSIS

"What Extent Parliament's Authority" (p. 165)
1. From what you know about early Massachusetts, would you agree with Hutchinson's or the assembly's initial comments? Why?
2. Does Hutchinson see a possible compromise between the notion of Parliamentary supremacy and colonial demands? Does the assembly believe that such a compromise is possible?
3. Why does Hutchinson use the words "grant and charter" and the assembly use the words "parties to the compact"?

MAP EXERCISE

"The Changing Deployment of British Troops, 1763–1775" (pp. 174–175)
1. What was the main purpose of the British troop deployment in 1763?
2. How did this purpose change during the next three years? Why were there new garrisons in the South and Southwest?
3. What was the main purpose of British strategy in 1775? Where had British forces been reduced?

ILLUSTRATION ANALYSIS

"The Battle of Lexington" (p. 176)
1. The caption says that British troops panicked at Lexington. Does this painting suggest that a panic occurred?
2. Are any of the colonial "Minutemen" firing back at the British? Do you believe this?
3. What do you suppose were the political loyalties of the artist?

CHAPTER CONTEXT

The previous chapter discussed the increasing influence of Europe in the colonies and explored conflicts between the back country and seaboard areas in North America.

This chapter describes the evolving determination of Parliament to assert greater authority over the American colonies. Both mother country and colonies debated the proper relationship between the two. The colonies asserted their right to self-determination, while Parliament finally settled on the policy of strict control of colonial affairs. The decision to enforce revenue laws for the colonies provoked violent resistance to British policy. Rather than seek a compromise solution, Parliament sent troops to enforce its policies. The Continental Congress responded by forming a colonial army, and the clashes at Lexington and Concord inaugurated the War of American Independence.

The next chapter will consider the course of the war and its outcome.

7

War, Revolution, and the New Political Order

OUTLINE AND SUMMARY

I. Toward Independence

A. Civil War

Although rebellion was on the rise in the colonies, many Americans remained loyal to the British government. These loyalists consisted of those whose fortunes were tied directly to the British; wealthy, conservative Americans who could not stomach the democratic ideals of the rebels; and rural families who opposed the patriots because of long-held grievances. At the Second Continental Congress, the loyalists were barely outnumbered by the patriots, but King George III refused to use this division among the colonists to increase the chances of suppressing the rebellion. As the struggle escalated, demands for independence from Britain became more widespread. To break with the monarchical system required a questioning of the hierarchical nature of American social and family structure. Thomas Paine's *Common Sense* provided an ideological basis for independence, and, on July 4, 1776, the Continental Congress unanimously approved the Declaration of Independence.

B. The Fortunes of War

The well-trained British army was able to drive the American forces into retreat from the seaboard areas. Although the colonial army was able to win few battles, its will to continue the struggle was strong. The poorly trained and equipped Americans were held together by the inspirational leadership of General George Washington. The British proceeded cautiously, realizing that a major defeat would bring to an end the campaign to suppress the rebels. The French, long-time enemies of the British, joined with American forces and provided experienced leadership and financial assistance. By the time the British were ready to make concessions to the colonists in order to return to the "condition of 1763," there was little hope of reconciliation. French and Spanish involvement expanded the colonial rebellion into a European struggle as well.

C. Victory at Yorktown

Having lost the battle for New England, the British turned their attention to the South. After initial victories in South Carolina, the British began to lose ground to the patriot forces. Finally, with the aid of French troops and a French naval blockade off the coast of Virginia, the Americans were able to surround and defeat the British forces at Yorktown, bringing an end to the fighting. The Americans won the war largely because it was fought thousands of miles from the home base of the British and in a countryside widely supportive of the rebellion.

II. The Disruptions of War

A. War, Inflation, and Debt

All aspects of colonial society were disrupted by the war. Long-standing conflicts within colonial society often flared into violence during the struggle. Both urban and rural economies suffered because of the presence of the British army and the devastation wrought by the fighting. A major difficulty for the Americans was financing the war effort. Congress issued currency to cover expenses, and the use of this volatile paper money enriched speculators and led to dangerous inflation. Soldiers paid with government paper suffered because its value depreciated. The war brought financial chaos to the new nation's economic system.

B. Republicanism Debated

The independence movement in Pennsylvania led to the creation of a democratic-republican state constitution in which artisans played a major role. There were three sources for the radical democracy embodied in this document: the artisans' belief in the labor theory of value, evangelical religion, and the intellectual leadership of people like Thomas Paine. The Pennsylvania elite opposed the leveling implications of this development and began to seek a revision of the new state constitution. Throughout the colonies, the elites began to challenge and successfully overturn the democratic-republican documents that had emerged in the midst of the war. The American aristocracy saw to it that the interests of the privileged classes would be protected in the new constitutions. This was ensured by the establishment of property qualifications for voting and officeholding. Nevertheless, the institutions of the new nation provided for expressions of the popular will and recognized that republicanism required a measure of social and economic, as well as political, equality.

III. Property and the New Social and Political Order

A. Liberty and Property

Along with life and liberty, the colonists fought for the right to private property. The ownership of property, usually in the form of land, became a requirement for political participation in most of the new states. When loyalist property was confiscated, it was sold to raise revenue, not to provide for a wider distribution of wealth. After a short period of radical democracy, the colonial elite reestablished its control in the new states. Women had hoped, in vain, that the new republican ideology would alter the patriarchal system in American law. The democratic ideas of the period did have an impact on the institution of slavery, though. The northern states embarked on a course of gradual emancipation but did not embrace the notion of racial equality. In the South, on the other hand, the fierce debate over slavery did not bring an alteration in the system. Many slaves had received their freedom during the struggle for independence, but the rise of the cotton culture in the southern states ended the possibility of peaceful emancipation there.

B. Property and Politics

The economic chaos brought about by the War of Independence was not eased by the transition to peace. Political struggles broke out over the issues of raising taxes and dealing with indebtedness. While those without property had little influence, artisans and back-country farmers began to compete with the seaboard elites for control of the new legislatures. Several of the states took steps to ease the plight of debtors. Massachusetts refused to do so, and many farmers in the middle and western parts of the state revolted under the leadership of Daniel Shays and sought relief through violent action. Shays' Rebellion caused a conflict in the minds of many patriots who supported the notion of popular resistance but rejected the movement's attacks on property.

C. The Whig Constitutional Triumph

Several elements of the population favored a stronger central government than the one provided by the Articles of Confederation—for example, conservative Whigs and officials who had played national roles during the war. In 1787 a convention was called to revise the Articles. Many of the delegates had nationalist sympathies, and they accepted James Madison's proposal to form a truly national government. Realizing that it was necessary to serve the interests of both large and small states, the delegates agreed to have a national legislature composed of two houses—one formed on the basis of population, and the other having equal representation from each state. The national executive would be independent of the legislature and indirectly elected. Slavery could continue, and each slave would count as three-fifths of a person for purposes of apportionment and taxation. The completed document gave power to the national government in many areas but retained some sovereignty for the states. The struggle over ratification divided the politicians into Federalists (proratification) and Anti-Federalists. The Federalists won the battle after agreeing to add the Bill of Rights to the document. The new government of the United States represented a victory for Whig republicanism, and the more radically democratic ideas of the revolutionary era had been subverted in the process.

ESSAY QUESTIONS

1. Compare and contrast the attitudes of loyalists and patriots in 1775–1776 over the goals of the colonial rebellion.
2. Describe the major campaigns of the War of American Independence. What reasons can you give for the American victory and British defeat?
3. What was the economic impact of the War of American Independence on the new nation? Discuss and evaluate the policies adopted to ease the financial plight of the population.
4. Discuss and evaluate the process whereby Pennsylvania adopted a "democratic-republican" state constitution in 1776.
5. What economic and political factors led to the enactment of Whig republican constitutions in several states in the late 1770s and early 1780s?
6. Discuss the debate over slavery that took place in the states during the revolutionary era. What policies were adopted as a result of these debates?
7. What were the economic and political factors that led to Shays' Rebellion?
8. What elements in the population felt the need for a stronger national government than that provided for by the Articles of Confederation? What did they do to pursue their goal?

9. What decisions did the Constitutional Convention of 1787 reach in resolving the conflicts that emerged in the debates?
10. Discuss and evaluate the arguments of the Federalists and Anti-Federalists over the issue of the ratification of the Constitution.

IDENTIFICATIONS

loyalists

Lord Dunmore

Common Sense

General William Howe

Battle of Saratoga

The "Swamp Fox"

Marquis de Lafayette

"not worth a continental"

democratic-republicanism

Thoughts on Government

Abigail Adams

Manumission Act of 1782

Gabriel Prosser

Shays' Rebellion

Northwest Ordinance of 1787

The Federalist Papers

PRIMARY SOURCE ANALYSIS

"The Massachusetts Courts Rule Slavery Is Unconstitutional" (p. 197)
1. According to the selection, was slavery a legal institution in colonial Massachusetts? What is the difference between an institution protected by "enactment" and one protected by "usage"?
2. What Enlightenment ideas are expressed in this passage? Was slavery declared illegal in Massachusetts because it runs counter to these ideas?
3. To what document does Cushing appeal? The Declaration of Independence? Articles of Confederation? Or what?

FIGURE ANALYSIS

"The Revolution and Political Democracy: Change in the Wealth of Elected Officials" (p. 199)
1. In which region was the change in the wealth of elected officials greatest after independence? Why?
2. These changes in the wealth of elected officials could have been produced in several different ways. First, rich men could have lost their offices to poor men. Second, the states could have decided to elect many minor officials who had once been appointed. Or, third, an end to the common practice of allowing individuals to hold several offices simultaneously could have opened political careers to many more

individuals. Based on your reading of this chapter, which of these processes do you think was most important?

3. What would you conclude from this chart about the democratization of officeholding as a result of the War of American Independence?

ILLUSTRATION ANALYSIS

"An American Recruiting Poster" (p. 185)
1. According to this poster, who is the United States at war with?
2. The poster uses the words "troops, now raising." Why?
3. Compare the figures in this poster to the "Minutemen" in the painting on page 176 and to the riflemen pictured on page 188. What do the differences tell you about General Washington's task?

CHAPTER CONTEXT

The previous chapter explored the increasing tension between the colonies and Great Britain in the 1760s and 1770s and concluded with the outbreak of war.

This chapter carries the story of the War of American Independence to the conflict's successful conclusion. The devastating economic impact of the military struggle is described, as are the faltering attempts to restore financial stability to the new nation. As new state governments came into existence, the initial, radically democratic thrust was tempered by the restoration to power of the colonial elites in most states. The widely felt need for a stronger central government led to the adoption of the Constitution of 1787 as the basic document of American political life and the establishment of Whig republicanism as the dominant political philosophy of the United States.

The next chapter will describe the political debates that emerged in the new nation and their implications for national development.

8

The Political World:
Commercial Enterprise
and Westward
Expansion

OUTLINE AND SUMMARY

I. The Political Crisis of the 1790s

A. Hamilton Versus Jefferson

After his election to the presidency in 1789, George Washington established the cabinet system and appointed Thomas Jefferson as secretary of state and Alexander Hamilton as secretary of the treasury. Hamilton developed policies that favored the commercial elite and moneyed interests of the new nation. In order to establish firm national credit, he proposed that the government redeem Confederation securities at face value, thereby enriching speculators, and recommended that the central government assume the remaining war debts of the states. Jefferson and James Madison opposed Hamilton's policies, arguing that they would work to the disadvantage of artisans, yeomen, and ex-soldiers. The proposal to charter a national bank led to a disagreement on whether the Constitution should be interpreted strictly or loosely. Washington's support of Hamilton's policies usually led to their adoption by Congress. Jefferson broke with the administration and began to form an opposition political party. Hamilton continued to organize the nation's fiscal affairs, advocating that the government support the development of manufacturing. Jefferson and his supporters, on the other hand, hoped to see the United States develop as a nation of yeoman farmers and artisans, with its wealth built on agriculture. For a hundred years the nation followed both paths, undergoing revolutions in both industry and agriculture.

B. War and Politics

The French Revolution and the subsequent war between France and Britain had a major impact on American life in the 1790s. The war in Europe stimulated trade, and the United States climbed out of the recession of the postwar years. The American merchant marine became one of the world's largest, carrying goods to all the warring parties. The republican revolution in France was initially greeted enthusiastically by Americans, but, as a result of later developments there, the Jeffersonian Democratic-Republicans continued to support the revolution, but the American mercantile elite turned against what it saw as democratic excesses. Federalist support for France's opponents faltered when Great Britain began seizing American ships bound for French ports. The Jay treaty of 1795 enabled Washington's administration to avert on open break with Britain and provided the Democratic-Republicans with further reason to oppose the pro-British policy of the Federalists.

C. The First Party System

The election of 1796 brought the First Party System into active participation in electoral politics. Although the Founding Fathers had hoped to avoid this development, sharp disagreement over Federalist policy led to the emergence of a coherent opposition. The rudimentary structure of party politics is reflected in the fact that, in 1796, the Federalists captured the presidency with their candidate, John Adams, while the Republican Jefferson became vice-president. The Adams administration sought to retard the growth of the Jeffersonian party by adopting the Alien and Sedition Acts. The Republicans responded with the Kentucky and Virginia resolutions, which attacked the abuse of federal power and supported states' rights. Running against Federalist policies, Jefferson won the presidency in 1800, and a peaceful transition—"the Revolution of 1800"—took place.

II. Westward Expansion

A. Migration and Agricultural Change

Migrants from New England and the South flooded into the area between the Appalachians and the Mississippi River. The southerners were fleeing the elite-dominated Chesapeake region in search of yeoman status, while the New Englanders moved to find enough decent farmland for their surplus population. The loss of farm labor in the East and South led to the adoption of new agricultural methods and crops in those regions, contributing to an increase in agricultural productivity and farm income.

B. *The Transportation Bottleneck*

As settlement of the trans-Appalachian West increased, the problem of transportation in the new nation became more evident. It was difficult for farmers to get their crops to market without a more fully developed transportation system. Only those farmers near navigable rivers were able to move their goods efficiently. States undertook to build roads and canals in order to reduce shipping costs. The lack of transportation tended to make western farm life dependent on a barter system within local areas and encouraged home manufactures. The states and the federal government adopted a variety of approaches in the marketing of public lands. In this process, land companies and speculators were able to reap enormous profits. The cost of land to potential freeholders fell under Republican administrations but still remained out of reach for many farmers. Even in the West, then, farm families would remain in debt until the development of an economically viable system of transportation.

C. *The Native American Challenge*

The Treaty of Paris (1783) ceded the British possessions east of the Mississippi and south of the Great Lakes to the United States. Many Indian tribes formerly allied with the British lived in that territory, and, in order for the Americans to take possession of the land, they had to fight the Indians. The threat of military action brought some tribes to the bargaining table and freed some land for settlement. The Shawnee, under Tecumseh and his brother the Prophet, sought to form an Indian federation to resist the westward advance of the American population. A revival of Indian spirituality fueled the federation movement, but the defeat of Indian forces at the Battle of Tippecanoe in 1811 ended Tecumseh's dream. But Indians throughout the West now realized that they would have to fight if they were going to retain their lands.

III. The Republicans in Power

A. *Jefferson as President*

Jefferson appointed politicians from Federalist areas to office in an attempt to broaden the appeal of the Republican party. Congress repealed legislation that had allowed the Federalists to dominate the newly established federal judiciary, but John Marshall, the Federalist chief justice of the Supreme Court, was able to establish the right of judicial review through a carefully circumscribed decision in the case of *Marbury v. Madison* (1803). The Jefferson administration proceeded to dismantle certain elements of the Federalist legislative program; the Alien and Sedition Acts were allowed to lapse, and a fiscal program altering Hamilton's policy of increasing federal indebtedness was undertaken. In attempting to secure the port of New Orleans for American trade, Jefferson was offered the chance to purchase all of Louisiana from France. Although doubtful of his constitutional rights in this matter, Jefferson felt he could not overlook this opportunity and, at a stroke, almost doubled the size of the United States. Leading Federalists opposed this expansion, and secessionist conspiracies were exposed. The rapid expansion of the nation led to increased sectional and political conflict.

B. Crisis at Sea

The Napoleonic Wars in Europe revived a longstanding maritime conflict between the United States and Great Britain. Both France and Britain forbade neutral vessels, under threat of confiscation, from trading with their enemies. In a more direct affront to American sovereignty, British warships stopped merchant vessels and seized (impressed) British-born seamen to serve in their navy. In order to protect American shipping and in hopes of bringing to an end the European attacks on neutral trading, Jefferson passed the Embargo Act of 1807, which prohibited American ships from trading with any nation. When this policy proved unsuccessful, Madison, who had become president in 1808, had it repealed and open, though risky, trade resumed. In the meantime, Americans were agitating for the annexation of Florida, which belonged to Britain's ally Spain. Representatives from the western states proposed military action to achieve this end. Madison persuaded Congress to declare war with Britain in 1812, ostensibly to protect the American West and gain respect for neutral rights in the Atlantic. Since Federalist merchants and seamen opposed the war, however, one must look to the "war hawks" of the frontier for the actual causes of the conflict.

C. The War of 1812

The fighting in the War of 1812 was sporadic and inconclusive for two years. In New England, Federalist opposition to the war was expressed in the Hartford convention, which called for a drastic overhaul of the Constitution to limit the power of the western states. In 1814, with the defeat of Napoleon, Great Britain decided to seek a negotiated settlement of the war in America as well. The Treaty of Ghent resolved none of the issues that had precipitated the war, but it did put an end to the fighting. Ironically, the only major battle won decisively by either side was fought after the peace treaty had been signed: General Andrew Jackson's forces defeated the British garrison in the Battle of New Orleans. Although the victory had no impact on the outcome of the war, it catapulted Jackson into national prominence and restored a measure of pride to the American people.

ESSAY QUESTIONS

1. Compare and contrast the views and policies of Hamilton and Jefferson on the appropriate way to develop the American economy.
2. What impact did events in Europe in the 1790s have on the United States?
3. What factors led to the emergence of political parties in the new nation?
4. Discuss and evaluate the Alien and Sedition Acts passed during the Adams administration.
5. What conditions led southerners and northerners to migrate west of the Appalachians? What impact did this migration have on agriculture in the seaboard states?
6. How was public land distributed to settlers in the areas opened up for settlement by the Treaty of Paris (1783)?
7. As Americans moved west, what policies were followed in dealing with Indian tribes in the areas of settlement?
8. In what ways did the policies of the Republican administration of Jefferson differ from the previous Federalist legislative programs?
9. Discuss and evaluate the continuing controversy between the United States and European nations. How did Jefferson attempt to resolve this issue? Evaluate the result of his efforts.
10. Discuss the causes of the War of 1812, and evaluate the results of that struggle. Did the United States win or lose the war?

IDENTIFICATIONS

"Report on Manufactures"
"elastic clause" of the Constitution
The Wealth of Nations
Northwest Ordinance of 1787
Edmund Genêt
Jay treaty
X, Y, and Z
Sedition Act

Aaron Burr
"Revolution of 1800"
"bootstrap" settlement
Tecumseh
John Marshall
Lewis and Clark
"war hawks"
Battle of New Orleans

PRIMARY SOURCE ANALYSIS

"A Pottawatomie Chief on the Battle of Tippecanoe" (p. 230)
1. What had General Harrison said that so offended some of the Indians?
2. What was the primary reason the Indians lost the battle, according to Chief Shabonee? Evaluate his explanation.
3. Why do you think the young Indians were so convinced the whites could easily be defeated?

MAP EXERCISE

"Settlement Patterns in the Northwest Territory" (p. 225)
1. What do you think are the advantages and disadvantages of the rectangular survey method of dividing the land?
2. What shifts in American political life are reflected in the changes in the conditions attached to the direct purchase of federal land?
3. Is the pattern of land distribution any more egalitarian in one area than in another?

ILLUSTRATION ANALYSIS

"A New Western Farm" (p. 221)
1. In the area pictured here, which land has been cleared first? Why?
2. Does the picture show one farm or several?
3. What is the white man in the canoe at the left doing? What is the Indian in the same canoe doing? What does this picture suggest about Indian-white relations in the Northwest?

CHAPTER CONTEXT

The previous chapter described the successful completion of the War of American Independence and the establishment of the system of government based on the Constitution of 1787.

This chapter explains how the political party system emerged out of the conflicting ideas of Alexander Hamilton and Thomas Jefferson. The Federalists tried to suppress the Democratic-Republicans through fiscal and political policy. On the verge of war throughout the 1790s, the nation was the victim of conflicts in Europe. After Jefferson was elected president in 1800, the Republicans repealed much of the Federalist program. Jefferson adopted trade restrictions in an attempt to force Great Britain and France to allow Americans freedom of the seas. The maritime issue provided an excuse for the "war hawks" to initiate the War of 1812. This struggle almost split the nation, as New England Federalists vigorously opposed the war effort. The peace settlement of 1814 restored the status quo of 1812 but left a bitterly divided nation.

The next chapter explores the gradual development of a national identity in the first third of the nineteenth century.

9

A Mature Preindustrial Society

OUTLINE AND SUMMARY

I. The Subject Races

A. *The Fate of the Native Americans*

Americans saw the Indian tribes as backward peoples who would have to fall before the march of civilization. Efforts were made—unsuccessfully, for the most part—to transform the Native Americans into Christian farmers. Most Indian leaders resisted this policy, arguing that the races should remain entirely separate. Some Indians, on the other hand, sought to blend European and Indian beliefs into new cultural patterns. The traditional Indian way of life, based on the clan and matrilinear descent, varied sharply from the European patterns and discouraged assimilation. One major exception to this maintenance of Indian tradition was the movement among mixed-blood Cherokees to follow American economic and cultural styles. Their decision to adopt the patterns of white farmers did not, however, make them acceptable to the Americans and only further alienated them from their full-blood brothers.

B. *The Expansion of Slavery*

Thirteen percent of the Afro-American population in the United States was free, and in the northern cities they formed a variety of community organizations—churches, schools, lodges, and so on. Hundreds of thousands of Africans were imported into the South between

1789 and the closing of the slave trade in 1808. As the slave population grew in size, however, more of the increase was due to natural reproduction than importation. The growth of the cotton culture in the new states of the Southwest led to the sale of slaves from older sections of the country to the farming frontier in Alabama and Mississippi. The growth of slavery in the expanding nation brought a political crisis that was resolved by the Missouri Compromise of 1820, which restricted the expansion of slavery in the Louisiana Territory to its southern portion.

C. Afro-American Society and Culture

As the slave trade died out, the African influence on Afro-American culture decreased. Blacks began to borrow elements of the white way of life to merge with aspects of their remembered past. Although owners would not recognize the legality of slave marriage, the black community developed its own forms of family life, including incest taboos and tightly knit kinship patterns. Most slaves on southern plantations lived in stable family units, and, when the sale of a spouse away from the plantation took place, new family units were formed. By the nineteenth century, the excessive brutality of the slave system was softened as a result of republican ideology and Christian piety. Slaveowners began to adopt a patriarchal attitude toward their bondsmen. Instead of "savages" to be "tamed," the slaves became "children" to be "nurtured." Slaves took advantage of this change in attitude to demand certain rights—regular holidays and the establishment of a "task" system, for example. Some slaves continued to resist the system with violence, but most saw revolt as a futile response to their condition. Christianity became the dominant religion of the slave community, but the slaves developed their own interpretation of the Biblical message of resistance and redemption.

II. The Formation of Social Identity

A. Regional Cultures

The regional cultures of early America persisted into the nineteenth century. New England communities were seen as religious, industrious, educated, and close-knit. Southerners were viewed as rowdy and uneducated. In the middle states, ethnic identity remained particularly strong. People from the seaboard areas who moved west took their regional culture with them, but in time a western identity began to emerge. Only the elite worked toward establishing a national culture.

B. Education and Society

New England provided its children with a widespread network of public schools, while elsewhere in the new nation primary education was limited to a few private institutions. Nationwide, few children went to high school and fewer still to college. There was little intellectual culture, and Washington Irving was the only American author known in Europe. In order to standardize American English, Noah Webster published dictionaries and spelling books. The attempt to form a national public educational system failed, but in the 1820s leaders in eastern states promoted public schools for the shaping of character. The elite continued to prefer their own private institutions, while farmers and artisans supported public primary schools for the teaching of basic reading, writing, and arithmetic.

C. Religion Versus Reforms

Virginia took the lead in separating church and state and in endorsing freedom of conscience in spiritual affairs. But many religious leaders in the new nation thought there should be one state church, supported by the national government. Many states gave full political rights only to Protestants, and some states maintained established churches for several decades into the nineteenth century. The Bill of Rights dealt only with a *national* establishment of religion and left the states to formulate their own policies in this area. Rationalists, many of whom were deists, opposed state interference in religious affairs and were accused of promoting atheism. After the War of Independence, the most democratically organized churches—the Methodists and Baptists—grew dramatically, while the hierarchically structured Episcopal church declined.

III. The Mature Preindustrial Economy

A. Merchant Capitalism

The wars in Europe around the turn of the century gave American merchants a chance to reap fortunes through foreign trade. The expansion of American commerce was aided by the development of a stable banking system, which was able to provide loan capital. Merchants not only looked abroad for profit but also began to expand domestic manufacturing through the putting-out system. Entrepreneurs provided raw materials for household manufactures and marketed the finished products. Rural families in New England and the middle states involved themselves eagerly in this process, becoming both artisans and farmers at the same time. Sections of rural society began growing crops and raising livestock to provide the materials for the expanding household manufacturing system. Barter ceased playing a dominant role in the rural economy, as the availability of cash led to a diversification of the rural market system. The standard of living of Americans rose steadily through the first third of the century, and a self-sufficient American nation emerged from this process.

B. A Transformation in the Law

In the early period of national development, state legislatures played a much larger role in the people's lives than the federal government did. The states encouraged economic progress by chartering corporations and building roads between market centers. Government was seen as an active, not a passive, institution, creating and expanding economic opportunity. Statute law began to take precedence over the common law in the development of the new governmental system. The conflict between the states and the national judiciary can be seen most clearly in the work of John Marshall, chief justice of the Supreme Court. Marshall insisted on the predominance of federal over state law, the maintenance of traditional property rights, and the theory of judicial activism. Through a series of landmark cases, Marshall was able to carry out his judicial philosophy.

ESSAY QUESTIONS

1. Discuss the development of policies for dealing with the Indian population in the new nation. How did the Indian population resist these policies?
2. What important changes in the slavery system took place in the early nineteenth century? What issues led to the adoption of the Missouri Compromise?
3. Discuss and evaluate the development of Afro-American culture within the institution of slavery.
4. How did the emergence of a "paternalistic" attitude toward slavery affect the relationship between masters and slaves?
5. Compare and contrast the three main regional cultures: New England, middle states, and South.
6. Discuss and evaluate the place of educational institutions in the United States during this period. What was seen as the main functions of the schools?
7. Analyze the arguments presented for and against the policy of the separation of church and state in the new nation.
8. Discuss the development of the system of household manufacturing in the United States. What impact did this system have on rural America?
9. How did the new states encourage economic development within their borders?
10. Discuss the legal and governmental impact of the major Supreme Court cases presided over by John Marshall.

IDENTIFICATIONS

Sequoyah

AME churches

"personal liberty" laws

Missouri Compromise

"task" system

Nat Turner

Uncle Sam

Washington Irving

Noah Webster

Isaac Backus

John Jacob Astor

Bank of the United States

eminent domain

McCulloch v. Maryland

Fletcher v. Peck

Dartmouth College v. Woodward

PRIMARY SOURCE ANALYSIS

"A Chief's Understanding of Religion" (p. 244)

1. Whom do you think Red Jacket is speaking to? What do you think he means by "Brother"?
2. What is Red Jacket's reason for thinking that the "Great Spirit" did not mean for the Indians to follow the "book"?
3. What does Red Jacket think are the main differences the "Great Spirit" made between his "white and red children"?

MAP EXERCISE

"The Missouri Compromise" (p. 248)

1. If slavery was to be prohibited north of 36°30' latitude, how many new slave states do you think could be created in the area shown on this map as U.S. territory?
2. How many new free states would you predict might be formed?
3. If you were a proslavery senator, why would you have accepted a compromise that apparently left so limited an area for the expansion of slavery?

ILLUSTRATION ANALYSIS

"The 'Civilized' Cherokee" (p. 245)

1. What kind of audience do you think Sequoyah was posing for when he sat for this portrait?
2. Would you call the pipe Sequoyah is smoking a "white" object or a Native American one? Why?

3. What features in the painting mark Sequoyah as a Cherokee? What features suggest an integration of white civilization?

CHAPTER CONTEXT

The previous chapter discussed the emergence of political parties in the new nation and the impact of settlement in the trans-Appalachian West.

In this chapter, attempts of white Americans to establish firmer control over the nation's nonwhite population are explored. Both Indian and Afro-American peoples resisted the efforts to eradicate their cultures but with varying degrees of success. Regional variations in the new nation continued the preindependence pattern, and a western identity began to emerge across the mountains. The place of religion in the new nation remained controversial, with some Protestants seeking government support for their institutions. As financial and business institutions began to grow stronger, the merchant community was able to expand its activities into household manufacturing, transforming sections of rural America in the process. An activist federal judiciary under the leadership of Chief Justice John Marshall established federal supremacy in judicial affairs and set important precedents in the area of contract law.

The next chapter will further explore the developing American culture as a more democratic political system emerged.

10

Toward a New Culture

OUTLINE AND SUMMARY

I. The Dimensions of Public Culture

A. *A New Political Spirit*

The end of the War of 1812 saw the decline of Federalist fortunes and the end of the First Party System. Former Federalists began to join factions of the Republican party and make new political lives for themselves. John Quincy Adams, for example, became secretary of state under President James Monroe and was instrumental in establishing the southern, western, and northern boundaries of the United States through a series of critical treaties. In 1823, Monroe announced that the Western Hemisphere was closed to European colonization. As the traditional elite became less powerful in political affairs, the democratic spirit led to a broadening of the franchise. Except in four states, property qualifications for voting had been eliminated throughout the nation by 1820. More and more politicians began to emerge from the growing number of lawyers who achieved prominence through brilliant oratory both in court and in political campaigns.

B. *The Business Class*

At the turn of the century, most whites in the country shared elements of a common life. In rural areas all farmers had the same concerns—crops, livestock, weather, for example. Although there were class distinctions based on wealth or income, relationships across class

57

lines were often friendly and cooperative. In the early nineteenth century, however, the commercial elite began to set itself off from the rest of the society in a "business class," and a distinctly separate business-class culture began to take shape. Perhaps the most distinctive element of this new culture was the justification of an unlimited pursuit of wealth for its own sake. In establishing itself as a cultural arbiter, the business class initiated a campaign against the drinking of alcoholic beverages. This "temperance" movement drove a wedge between the business and working classes. An increase in the number of household domestics was another symptom of class distinctions. To increase and control their wealth, prominent families married their children either to cousins or to the offspring of other well-to-do families, creating networks of wealth and power. The business class sought to create an entire society in which the values of hard work and temperance would be dominant, but they were not willing to share their wealth in the process. So the early nineteenth century saw the creation of a society in which one class had political power and another had economic power.

C. Mechanics and Workers

The self-conscious formation of the business class led other groups in society to organize around their own self-interest. In the early nineteenth century, artisans began to form associations to pursue their class interests. As master craftsmen expanded their operations and entered the business class, their employees began to organize craft unions to protect their economic position. Workers coming from rural areas refused to submit to the time-work discipline of urban shops and resisted attempts to establish rigid controls over their working and private lives. The wages of unskilled workers in this period were barely sufficient to support subsistence, and the conditions of the workplace and nutritional deficiencies caused serious health hazards. Formerly good-natured celebrations crossing class lines were transformed into violent confrontations between competing religious, racial, and/or economic segments of society.

II. Changing Private Identities

A. The Conjugal Family

In the preindustrial period, most marriages were arranged by parents who felt themselves better prepared to make such momentous decisions than their immature offspring. As the nation grew, however, parents began to lose control of their children's lives. The growth of sentimentality—an emphasis on feeling—also altered marriage patterns. Love became a more important element than economics in seeking a marriage partner. While this may have provided a satisfactory relationship for some, the rise in the divorce rate indicated that romance alone was not sufficient to guarantee a lasting alliance. As more and more young couples moved from their hometowns to establish themselves, young women were deeply affected by the loss of family relationships. If the husband could not supply her emotional needs, the wife found herself neglected and alone.

B. Patterns of Child Raising

In the nineteenth century, family size began to decline in the United States as a result of several factors—among them the practice of birth control and a later marriage age for women. With fewer children, families began to focus more attention on their upbringing. The Calvinist practice of harsh discipline began to decline in this period, and the rationalist tradition of nurturing combined with the sentimentality of the age to produce a child-rearing philosophy that focused on the early formation of conscience and self-expression through education. Women began to be seen as more important in the child-centered family emerging in this period, and divorce rulings sometimes placed the children in the care of the mother, in sharp contrast to previous practice.

C. Women's "Sphere"

Sex roles in preindustrial society were clear-cut for the most part; women were subordinate to men. Wives and daughters were excluded from public life and were seen as the "weaker" sex. In the revolutionary era, however, the republican ideology infected some women and led them to seek the liberty and equality that the new nation promised. Few men were willing to grant this request, and a hierarchical relationship between the sexes persisted. Religious leaders, however, led the way in expanding women's so-called sphere by giving them the responsibility for moral and religious education in society. Women began to play public roles in religious movements, both in the founding of new churches and in forming organizations dedicated to good works. By the 1820s, female associations concerned with a variety of social and spiritual issues had come into existence, and the sense of shared gender identity among women became widespread. One outcome of the increasing moral role of women was the decline in premarital sexual relationships. Educational institutions that would provide a sound religious education for women were founded during this period, and educated women began to replace men as teachers in the nation's primary schools. Although still highly restricted in the general society, women found their sphere gradually expanding.

III. The Creation of the American National Character

A. *The Second Great Awakening*

The camp meeting revivals of the early nineteenth century transformed the nature of American religious life. The emotional preaching of Methodist and Baptist ministers in the back country led to the formation of many new congregations, as those denominations quickly became the largest Protestant churches in the United States. The new evangelical churches did not focus on learned discourse or the splitting of theological hairs but on intense religious feeling and a sense of mission. Many interdenominational agencies were formed that had as their goal the conversion of the entire nation to Protestant evangelical Christianity. While there were thoughtful intellectual developments among religious Americans—Unitarianism, for example, or the theologies of Samuel Hopkins and Lyman Beecher—most of the spiritual energy of the United States was directed toward personal conversion. When some of the awakened Christians got involved in movements for social reform, they were warned by their colleagues that they had strayed from their specific mission. There was some talk of forming a Christian political party to ensure that only followers of Jesus would be elected to public office.

B. *The National Character*

European travelers in the United States were fascinated by what they saw as a sharp contrast between the hierarchical structure of their home countries and the social mobility available to Americans. Seeing the republican ideology as the underlying principle, they believed that the economic opportunity that the growing nation presented was undermining the establishment of a rigid class system. Alexis de Tocqueville called the American pattern "individualism" and commented on the ambiguity it created. By emphasizing individual achievement, Americans neglected more communal values, such as cooperation and familial relationships. It is also important to note that a large number of Americans—blacks, Indians, women, and many white males—were not really free to participate in the competition that characterized economic development in the United States. But it became clear that a new American culture, based on republicanism, capitalism, and Christianity, was transforming the national life.

ESSAY QUESTIONS

1. What political patterns emerged from the decline of the First Party System? What directions did Republican policy take in the 1810s and early 1820s?

2. What impact did the legal profession have on political life in this period?
3. Discuss and evaluate the emergence of the business class in American society. How did this class seek to dominate the institutions of American life?
4. What steps did artisans and laborers take to try to resist the dominance of the business class?
5. What impact did the emergence of the culture of sentimentalism have on American family life?
6. Discuss and evaluate the changes in child-rearing practices during this period. Trace the emergence of the child-centered family.
7. In what ways and through what processes was women's "sphere" altered in the early nineteenth century?
8. Discuss and evaluate the impact of the Second Great Awakening on American religious and political life.
9. How did European visitors characterize American culture in the early nineteenth century? Evaluate their impressions.
10. What were the major elements contributing to the development of a new national character in the early nineteenth century? Indicate the most important events or individuals involved in this process.

IDENTIFICATIONS

Era of Good Feeling
Monroe Doctrine
Henry Clay
charivari
temperance movement
Boston Brahmins
Callithumpians
sentimentalism

conjugal family
women's "sphere"
Mary Wollstonecraft
"guardians of virtue"
Emma Willard
camp meeting revivals
circuit-rider
Alexis de Tocqueville

PRIMARY SOURCE ANALYSIS

"The Dilemmas of Womanhood, 1801" (p. 295)
1. Does Southgate accept the idea of a separate women's "sphere"? What do you think she means by this expression?
2. What specific restrictions on women would Southgate like to see lifted?
3. Does she think that education will cause women to resist their subordination?

MAP EXERCISE

"The Expansion of White Male Suffrage" (p. 283)
1. Did any state admitted between 1800 and 1830 have property qualifications for voting?
2. Using the map on page 248 as a guide, count the new slave states admitted between 1800 and 1830 with universal white manhood suffrage. Do the same exercise for free states.
3. What do your answers to question 2 suggest about the relationship between slavery and the extension of the suffrage?

ILLUSTRATION ANALYSIS

"Benjamin Franklin's Triumph" (p. 285)
1. What sayings in this illustration represent the philosophy of the emerging business class?
2. What different occupations can you identify in this illustration?
3. Out of what materials is the building in the center of the illustration being constructed?

CHAPTER CONTEXT

The previous chapter explored the ways in which preindependence American culture began to change slowly as the life of the new nation got under way.

This chapter describes in detail the emergence of a distinctly American way of life. Politics became more democratic, while a sharp distinction emerged between the business class and the rest of society. The new class formulated a philosophy of capitalism calling for hard work and the avoidance of alcohol. Workers found themselves increasingly subjugated economically and tried to organize to protect what they saw as their rights. The notion of sentimentality led to an emphasis on affection in marriage and child raising, leading to a focus on the conjugal family. Although still severely restricted, women's sphere expanded to include a responsibility for moral and religious leadership in private relationships. The Second Great Awakening provided Protestants with a heightened sense of mission, along with the responsibility to make the new nation a Christian one. European visitors saw the emergence of economic individualism as a major element in the new American character.

The next chapter will analyze the impact of the Industrial Revolution on the American nation.

11

The Industrial Revolution

OUTLINE AND SUMMARY

I. Northeastern Industrialization

A. The Textile Industry

The success of the Industrial Revolution in eighteenth-century Britain threatened to delay the emergence of competitive American industry. But the clandestine departure of artisans from Britain to the New World and successful industrial espionage allowed Americans to copy and even improve upon British technology in textile manufacturing. Nevertheless, the low cost of labor in British industry continued to give imported fabrics a competitive edge in American markets. With the development of the Waltham Plan, however, the cost of American textile production began to decline. Thousands of young women from the rural countryside went to work in the mills of New England and provided the majority of textile workers in the area. Continued innovation in machine design and factory organization enabled New England textiles to gain a competitive advantage over imported fabrics by the early 1820s. Other industrial processes were copied from the British, and, by 1840, American industry was competitive with British manufacturing in every important product area.

B. Manufacturers and Skilled Workers

With the exception of the large New England mills, most manufacturing establishments in the United States in the early years were small and economically unstable. Unable to raise capital from wealthy Americans or banks, industrial entrepreneurs had to depend on family finances, and many of the early factories failed because of undercapitalization. More successful was the development of American artisans' inventive skills. The evolution of the machine-tool industry exemplified this process. Working at first at home and later in larger machine shops, artisans perfected the milling of tools used to produce machine parts that were identical and therefore replaceable. By 1840, the machine-tool industry allowed American manufacturers to produce complicated machines quickly and efficiently.

II. Market Expansion

A. Expanding Trade

The American export trade dropped sharply in the early nineteenth century, as producers expanded their domestic markets. There was an increase of trade both within and between regions as the national economy became more self-sufficient. An exception to this pattern was the South. Southern planters were still tied to Great Britain, to which they exported their cotton and from which they imported manufactured goods. In this sense, the South retained a colonial relationship with the former mother country, and the economic growth of the South did not contribute to the development of the national pattern.

B. Urban Growth

The growth of cities and towns was stimulated by the increase in manufacturing and the commerce it generated. Mill cities developed along the fall line, and the old seaport cities continued to grow. New York City took the lead in international trade and emerged as the nation's financial center. The opening of the Erie Canal in 1825 only increased the prominence of New York as America's leading commercial city. In the West, cities developed at critical points on rivers, canals, and the Great Lakes. Little manufacturing took place in the western cities, but they served as important market centers during the transportation revolution.

C. Farming New Land

The Industrial Revolution in Europe displaced rural populations, but, in the United States, the same development stimulated a growth in the farming sector of the economy. The center of the American population moved gradually westward through this period, and by 1840 more than a third of the American people lived west of the Appalachians. Farmers moved west for a variety of reasons: better land, cheaper farms, overcrowding in the East, and so on. Innovations in farm machinery—a new type of iron plow, for example—eased the farmers' burdens in breaking new land. The need for certain agricultural raw materials for the new manufacturing processes enabled farmers to turn a cash profit from their crops, further enabling them to purchase the factory-produced goods from back East. This type of interregional trade strengthened the national economy.

D. The Transportation Revolution

In the 1820s and 1830s, both state and federal governments cooperated in building a national transportation system connecting the seaboard states with the trans-Appalachian West. At first the system featured the construction of roads, but this process was soon replaced by the building of canals and railroads. Water transportation was cheap, and the construction of canals connecting the major river and lake systems of the middle states drastically reduced the cost of shipping freight. The invention of the steamboat only further improved the transportation system, especially in upstream travel. By 1840, the canal system reached its peak. After that, the railroad would revolutionize American transportation even further.

E. The New Business Corporation

States encouraged the formation of business corporations to advance regional and national economic goals. The limited liability corporation made it possible to raise large sums of capital from investors for the development of the growing transportation system. Almost no manufacturers or mercantile firms incorporated until after the Civil War. The courts defined the restrictions within which corporations could operate, particularly those limitations that dealt with the conflict between monopoly and free competition. For the most part, states favored open competition among corporations, and the charters they issued so indicated.

III. The Birth of Industrial Society

A. The Concentration of Wealth

Most Americans were able to increase their standard of living during the Industrial Revolution. Among the wealthy, the increase provided for the construction of lavish dwellings. Even the middle class was able to take advantage of new construction technologies—the "balloon-frame" house, for example—to improve their living conditions. The growing inequality in the distribution of wealth, however, further increased the gap between the rich and the poor. The new industrial elite improved its economic position rapidly through technological innovation and the establishment of still larger factories. The old merchant elite maintained its position through expanded trade and shrewd real estate investment. Since taxes were rarely levied on "intangible" property or inheritance, fortunes passed down through the generations. During the same period, artisans' wages increased at a rate much higher than that of unskilled labor. Since the cost of living went up at the same time, the poor found themselves relatively worse off while the rest of the nation was enjoying a surge of prosperity.

B. Access to Wealth

Although economic instability led to many instances of bankruptcy, the middle class grew rapidly in this period. By 1840, half of America's males over thirty had accumulated some wealth. Although there are some examples of individuals rising from poverty to great wealth, such cases were extremely rare. Most families who achieved prosperity did so only slowly, following the philosophy of the business class. It was difficult for people with no property to move very far up the economic ladder. Skilled workers might, with luck and a careful marshaling of resources, move into the middle class. Most wage laborers, on the other hand, were doomed to economic insecurity and a bleak future for themselves and their families.

C. Mobility Versus Community

The level of geographical mobility was high during the Industrial Revolution. Most of those who changed their residences went to new towns in the West seeking economic opportunity. People with established property moved much less often than the footloose young male workers who owned nothing but their labor. In the new cities of the West, a stable, property-owning class established itself quickly and took on the responsibility of guiding the fortunes of the new communities. They recruited "suitable" migrants to settle in their midst and married their daughters to the most successful of the new arrivals. In order to advance one's fortunes in the new cities, it helped to strike up alliances, either financial or marital, with the established property owners. In this way, the cities of the West came to be dominated by networks of prosperous early settlers.

D. The Plight of the Urban Workers

The growth of the factory system began to lead to social instability. Instead of the former style of household manufacturing, in which the master, journeymen, and apprentices worked and often lived side by side, the emergence of production on a larger scale led to a separation of workers from masters and to a deterioration of the common life. Employers in manufacturing establishments removed their employees from view and expressed less concern for their welfare. Residential patterns followed the pattern of the workplace, with laborers living in urban districts of crowded and substandard housing. Although all segments of the society lived within the walking city, there grew up sharper distinctions among the various neighborhoods. The economic uncertainty felt by the workers now isolated from the larger community led to an increase in their consumption of alcohol. Saloons became commonplace in the poorer neighborhoods, and public drunkenness contributed to outbreaks of social disorder. The wealthy complained about the riotous behavior of the working classes but were unable to see how the economic revolution that had so benefited themselves also played a role in undermining the psychological stability of the workers and contributed to their alienation from the larger society.

E. The Business Cycle and Economic Instability

The economic instability of early industrialization became obvious in the Panic of 1837. The British, still major investors in and trading partners with the United States, began to restrict investment and lower demand for cotton. The American business community fell on hard times as a result. Trade, farming, and manufacturing entered a period of decline with the loss of British credit. The depression lasted for six years, with prices falling almost 50 percent, investment dropping by a quarter, and unemployment soaring. By 1843, prices had dropped so low that consumer spending began to rise, and the nation slowly climbed out of its economic collapse. The interdependence of the American economy fostered by industrialization meant that a weakness in any sector would affect the entire system. But recovery led the country to ignore the structural problems of the industrial order and move bravely, if blindly, into the economic future.

ESSAY QUESTIONS

1. Through what means were American industrialists able to copy the machinery of British textile mills?
2. Describe and evaluate the Waltham and Fall River plans for reducing labor costs in the New England textile industry.
3. Discuss the development and evaluate the importance of the American machine-tool industry.
4. Trace the evolution of the port of New York as the center of American commercial enterprise.
5. Discuss and evaluate the impact of the canal and steamboat on American commerce.

6. Analyze the factors that led to the concentration of wealth during the Industrial Revolution. What happened to the workers at the lowest levels of the economy?
7. Discuss and evaluate the factors that increased or decreased opportunity for social mobility during the Industrial Revolution.
8. How do you account for the increase in geographical mobility during this period? In what ways did the new cities of the West use this mobility to give stability to their communities?
9. Discuss the psychological impact of the Industrial Revolution on unskilled urban workers. What did workers do to relieve their emotional distress?
10. In what ways did the Panic of 1837 illustrate the weaknesses of the American economic structure created by the Industrial Revolution?

IDENTIFICATIONS

Samuel Slater
Waltham Plan
Rockdale, Pennsylvania
machine tools
Eli Whitney
fall line
auction system
*Charles River Bridge v. Warren
     Bridge*

Erie Canal
"balloon frame"
"intangible" wealth
casual workers
cordwainers
"grog shops"
business cycle
Panic of 1837

PRIMARY SOURCE ANALYSIS

"Lucy Larcom on Her Early Days at Lowell" (p. 313)
1. Can you tell from this selection what Larcom's specific job was?
2. What did Larcom like best about working in the mill, according to this selection?
3. Why did some girls prefer working in the mill to working as "hired help"?

FIGURE ANALYSIS

"Inland Freight Rates" (p. 326)
1. What caused upstream river rates to plummet around 1824?
2. What kind of scale is used in the vertical axis? What is the visual effect of such a scale?

3. Which twenty-year period do you think witnessed the most important decline in transportation costs?

ILLUSTRATION ANALYSIS

"Construction of the Erie Canal" (p. 325)
1. What is being done with the huge blocks of stone along the banks of the canal?
2. What mechanical device is being used to raise and lower the stones?
3. What form of power is being used to move the stones?

CHAPTER CONTEXT

The previous chapter described the changing shape of the American character under the influence of the business class and the spread of sentimentality.

This chapter explores the Industrial Revolution and its impact on American culture. Technological innovation and entrepreneurial imagination helped to bring about sharp increases in productivity. The decision to staff the textile mills of New England with young women from the countryside significantly lowered the cost of labor and made American textiles competitive with British. The development of the machine-tool industry enabled factories to become larger and more complex. A transportation revolution featuring canals and steamboats made it possible for market cities to grow and prosper. While most Americans experienced a rise in their standard of living in this period, unskilled workers found themselves falling in economic status. The fluctuations of the business cycle made economic instability a common feature of American life and led to the further alienation of the lower classes.

The next chapter will deal with political affairs during the Industrial Revolution.

12

The Political Culture of Industrializing America

OUTLINE AND SUMMARY

I. The Rise of the Business Class

A. The Benevolent Empire

The business elite and the middle class began to join forces to control the behavior of the working classes. Religious institutions led in the attempt to instill moral discipline into the lives of the lower classes. The social reformers of the Benevolent Empire established regional and national organizations for the regulation of what they saw as antisocial or deviant behavior. Middle-class women were particularly active in helping poor women and children. Workers and spokesmen for the poor objected to the goals and patronizing attitude of the middle-class reformers.

B. Business-Class Revivalism and Reform

Middle-class reform took on revivalistic overtones under the influence of Charles Grandison Finney, who had developed a theology of conversion that announced that salvation was open to all. Finney's revivals swept New York state in the 1830s, achieving enormous success among the middle class. Converts were exhorted to establish moral discipline in their lives and to communicate the reasons for their changed behavior to others, particularly their employees. Craft-union members and the poor remained resistant to the revivalists' call to a new moral existence. The temperance movement expanded under the leadership of the evangelical reformers, and a new work ethic combining the Puritan notion of "calling" with Benjamin Franklin's ethic of success through industriousness came to typify the moral education of the period. The evangelical revivals of the 1830s provided a more coherent self-identity for the business class but did little to improve the lot, either spiritual or economic, of the poor and working classes.

C. *The Labor Alternative*

As the business class was organizing itself, workers began to feel that the only way they could improve industrial conditions was to organize as well. Skilled workers were able to gain some protection for their rights, but the unskilled cotton-mill employees were unsuccessful in striking against the mill owners. Skilled workers found themselves divided because of their differing responses to industrialization. Those workers whose skills were threatened by the new factories were primarily interested in defending their interests, while those whose work lay outside the industrial process—construction workers, for example— were more interested in improving working conditions for themselves. Employers condemned union activism as criminal behavior, but court decisions declared that labor organizations should be free to pursue their workplace objectives. The evangelical revivals, which stressed the unity of interest between employer and employee and an ethic of upward mobility through sober industry, helped to prevent the formation of unions. Uncertain employment after the Panic of 1837 and geographical mobility also deterred the emergence of a strong and unified labor movement.

II. The Challenge of Democratic Politics

A. *Political Parties in Industrial Society*

Politics became more democratic during this period, as more states removed restrictions on voting and more offices became open to popular election. The chaotic structure of the party system led politicians to seek to establish order through party discipline. In order to win national elections, however, candidates had to appeal to a broad base within the electorate, cutting across regional and class lines. In the election of 1824, Andrew Jackson was the most successful in following this policy, but his lack of a majority of the electoral vote allowed the victory to go to John Quincy Adams.

B. *The Birth of the Democratic Party*

Jackson took no chances in 1828. He put together a political campaign that appealed to almost every segment of the population. Making only vague promises about his plans, he ran against special interests and advocated an expansion of democracy. In the midst of the campaign, his segment of the Republican party took the name "Democrats" to emphasize the thrust of its policy. Jacksonians in the North and South opposed the Industrial Revolution and the American System, which was advocated as a means to promote industrialization. Southerners were pleased with Jackson's historic antagonism toward the Indians and saw him as one of their own; he also had the support of urban workers and the small farmers of the Northeast. Only the northern business class opposed him, but this group was routed in the election as Jackson scored an overwhelming victory.

C. The Jacksonian Presidency

When Jackson assumed office, he used the power of the presidency to strengthen his Democratic party. Adopting the policy of the rotation of government officeholders, he placed Democrats in positions of influence throughout the federal bureaucracy. This "spoils system" enabled him to reward loyal party members. His cabinet was composed of representatives of all segments of the new political movement, but he actually relied on an informal "kitchen cabinet" of friends and supporters for advice. The policies he advocated were meant to develop a nation of self-sufficient citizens free from the powerful interests being built up through concentrations of wealth and industrialization.

D. Jackson and the Native Americans

Jackson's plan for removing the Indians from the southeastern states had near universal approval from whites in the frontier areas. He believed that the Native Americans were savages who must not be allowed to stand in the way of the march of civilization. First he removed federal protection of the Indians guaranteed by government treaties. The states then declared all Indian land subject to sale to whites. The Indian Removal Act of 1830 offered land west of the Mississippi to Indians who would agree to move. Some accepted, but, when others refused to move, the army led them on a forced march to their new land in the winter of 1838, a journey that killed almost a quarter of their population through starvation or exposure. Although Chief Justice John Marshall had ruled Jackson's Indian policies unconstitutional, the Court had no power to enforce this judgment.

E. The Tariff and Nullification

The high tariff originally passed during the Adams administration finally led South Carolina to adopt a policy of nullification—that is, denying that a federal law is enforceable within its borders. The idea of nullification was based on a theory of states' rights going back to the Kentucky and Virginia resolutions and reformulated by John C. Calhoun. The nullification crisis led to a debate over the nature of the federal union in which Calhoun's position found little support. Jackson was prepared to use force to bring South Carolina into line, but a compromise tariff bill eased the pressure for nullification.

F. The Bank Veto

Jackson used his attack on the Second Bank of the United States to emphasize his opposition to the monied class and its institutions. Most Americans were unaware of the functions of central banking and the importance of the careful management of the money supply. Banks in general were seen as unproductive parasites, further enriching the wealthy and condemning the poor to eternal poverty. Proprietors of state banks were often resentful of the regulatory functions of the Second Bank. Jackson responded to an attempt to recharter the Bank with a veto message explaining that the Bank was a tool of the wealthy. He then destroyed the effectiveness of the Bank by removing federal deposits and placing them in selected state banks. Jackson won this "bank war," but reaction to his fiscal policies contributed significantly to the emergence of a coherent political opposition.

III. The Second Party System

A. Emergence of the Whigs

At first the politicians who called themselves "Whigs" were united only in opposition to Jackson's policies. All regions were represented in this movement, and Jackson's overwhelming victory for reelection in 1832 led them to formulate a political program for the future that might generate public support. They feared what they saw as the radical tendencies among some Jacksonians for the destruction of privilege and the redistribution of wealth.

B. Whig Ideology

Whigs believed that privilege emerged "naturally" from human society and that concentrations of wealth were necessary for the development of transportation, banking, and manufacturing—concerns essential to the national economy. The republicanism of the Whigs was expressed in the claim that America was a classless society in which social mobility was open to all. The Whigs were the political expression of the business class, and they insisted that labor and capital shared the same interests. They opposed Jacksonianism as socially divisive and illustrative of mob rule. As a political program, the Whigs favored Clay's

American System, which would use government power to strengthen the industrial sector. Calhoun and his southern colleagues, though united with the Whigs in opposition to Jackson, were wary of the new party's republican ideology; they believed instead that the nation should have a rigidly enforced class system, with sharp distinctions between capital and labor.

C. *The Whig Triumph*

Organizing rapidly in a variety of regions, the Whigs were able to gain control of the House of Representatives by 1836. Vice-President Martin Van Buren, Jackson's hand-picked successor, won the presidency easily that year, but a lackluster administration and the Panic of 1837 caused a falling away of his public support. In 1840, the Whigs ran a war hero, William Henry Harrison, on a platform of opposition to the Democratic administration. Harrison's victory indicated that the Second Party System was in place, with two relatively equal organizations competing for control of the political processes of the nation.

ESSAY QUESTIONS

1. Describe the composition of the Benevolent Empire and evaluate its program for social reform.
2. Describe the theological basis for Charles Grandison Finney's evangelistic crusades. Present evidence supporting the notion that Finney's revivals were a movement of the middle class.
3. How did the organizational efforts of skilled and unskilled workers differ during this period? Evaluate the impact of labor activism in the early Industrial Revolution.
4. What political and social factors contributed to the rise of the Democratic party?
5. What policy was adopted by Jackson's administration in dealing with American Indians? What were the ultimate effects of this policy?
6. What political issues were at stake in the nullification crisis of 1832? How was this crisis resolved?
7. How did the "bank war" illustrate the divergent political philosophies of Jackson and his opponents?
8. What parts did Daniel Webster of Massachusetts play in the Jacksonian drama—at what times did he appear, on what issues did he speak out, what party factions did he align with?

9. Discuss and evaluate the Whigs' political program for America's future.
10. What factors enabled the Whigs to win the presidential election of 1840?

IDENTIFICATIONS

middle class
Benevolent Empire
General Union for Promoting the
    Observance of the Chris-
    tian Sabbath
Charles Grandison Finney
ten-hour day
"labor theory of value"
Commonwealth v. Hunt

the "corrupt bargain"
American System
National Republicans
"spoils system"
"kitchen cabinet"
Trail of Tears
nullification
the "bank war"
William Henry Harrison

PRIMARY SOURCE ANALYSIS

"Jackson to the Cherokee and the Cherokee's Reply" (p. 358)
1. From what you know about the Cherokee, evaluate Jackson's characterization of them in this selection.
2. What does Jackson mean by the statement: "Circumstances that cannot be controlled, and which are beyond the reach of human laws, render it impossible that you can flourish in the midst of a civilized community"?
3. On what legal basis do the Cherokee reject Jackson's appeal?

FIGURE ANALYSIS

"Church Growth by Denomination, 1780–1860" (p. 347)
1. Compare this figure with the similar figure on page 130. What has happened to the Anglican church?
2. What do the marks near the top of the Baptist and Methodist columns for 1860 mean? What accounts for the sharp increase in these denominations' memberships in 1860?
3. Why do you think the Catholic church grew so rapidly between 1820 and 1860?

ILLUSTRATION ANALYSIS

"A Whig Cartoon" (p. 364) and "Andrew Jackson" (p. 357)
1. In the portrait of Jackson on page 357, what is on the chair at the lower right? Why? What is the building in the distance? Why is it so small?
2. Why is it particularly pertinent to Whigs that Jackson be clothed in a king's robe? What is the historical significance of the document in Jackson's left hand?
3. Which image of Andrew Jackson do you think is more historically accurate? Which image is more useful to the historian?

CHAPTER CONTEXT

The last chapter analyzed the impact of industrialization on American society.

This chapter describes the political history of the 1820s and 1830s, the period encompassing the Industrial Revolution. The business class used the revivals of Charles Grandison Finney to strengthen its work ethic among the larger population. Rejecting the leadership of the business class, skilled and unskilled workers organized themselves in an effort to improve their economic condition. Their lack of a unified approach weakened their position, however, and the labor movement collapsed during the Panic of 1837. The rise of the Jacksonian Democrats threatened the power of the business elite by restricting governmental economic activity on behalf of industrialization. Intense political activity by the new Whig party, on the other hand, led to the defeat of the Democrats in the presidential election of 1840.

The next chapter will explore further the significance of individualism in American culture and will continue the consideration of reform movements.

13

Individualism and Reform

OUTLINE AND SUMMARY

I. Intellectual Ferment in American Literature

A. Unitarianism and Transcendentalism

A new religious movement that emphasized the possibilities of human nature became the philosophy of the New England intellectual elite. Unitarianism liberated theology from the rigidity of the Calvinist tradition and focused on the necessity of freeing the human spirit through reason. Reason was not enough for some young thinkers, however, as they pursued a "transcendent" reality through feeling and an intuitive link with the natural world. The leading transcendentalist was Ralph Waldo Emerson, who popularized the new intellectual development through a series of widely read essays and well-attended lecture tours.

B. The Celebration of the Individual

The individualism that was an important part of the business and religious ethic of the Industrial Revolution received thoughtful treatment by writers in this period. Transcendentalism's stress on the solitary person in the midst of the natural world found impressive restatement in the literary works of Washington Irving and James Fenimore Cooper. Henry David Thoreau actually lived alone in the woods and described in intimate detail his spiritual quest for transcendence. Perhaps the most extravagant expression of the new individualism was found in the exuberant poetry of Walt Whitman. Of all those influenced by transcendentalism, only Whitman dealt openly with human sexuality and announced a thoroughgoing rejection of organized religion.

C. The Limits of Individualism

The darker side of individualism was explored by Nathaniel Hawthorne and Herman Melville. In *The Scarlet Letter*, the breaking of social taboos led to the death and degradation of the leading characters. The individual was not finally free to violate the norms of society without paying a high price. In Melville's *Moby Dick,* Captain Ahab's determined pursuit of his nemesis led not only to his own downfall but also to the destruction of the community of which he was the leader. The works of Melville, Thoreau, and Whitman were not popular with the middle-class reading public. Their explorations of the extreme limits of individualism found less favor than the more moderate analyses of Hawthorne and Emerson.

D. Perspectives from a "Separate Sphere"

Women formed the vast majority of the American reading public, so it should come as no surprise that female novelists were the best-selling writers of the period. These women authors focused on the problems of the individual woman in her natural community—the family. Accepting without question the notion of a separate, domestic sphere for women, these novelists claimed that women held a superior status to men—the responsibility for forming the moral character of their husbands and sons. In fact, however, women were not restricted merely to the home but were also active in religious and community life. They were not, on the other hand, to become involved in the sordid male worlds of business and politics. Ironically, the commercial success of the female writers very definitely involved them in the business world, but they did not explore this aspect of their lives in their writing. Many middle-class women did not feel that they were oppressed because they remained free to explore their individuality in their own specific sphere.

II. Communal Experiments

A. Brook Farm

Many individuals, rejecting the ethic of the business society, formed alternative communities during this period. They hoped to demonstrate by example that existence could be fulfilling without acquisitiveness. Massachusetts transcendentalists formed the community of Brook Farm, a lively settlement of artists, writers, and intellectuals. Unfortunately, Brook Farm had no economic base or productive facilities. When a reorganization required labor discipline, much of the enthusiasm of the inhabitants declined. It became clear that for a communal society to survive, a high level of disciplined work would be required. This was more likely to happen when the participants were from a less exalted social class than those at Brook Farm.

B. The Shakers

The Shaker religious movement, founded by Ann Lee Stanley, formed many successful communities in the 1820s and 1830s. The Shakers required the communal ownership of property, obedience to the church, abstinence, and celibacy. Sin could be overcome only through a dedication to the life of the community. Women played an equal role to men in governing the community, although a traditional division of labor was maintained. Through successful marketing of agricultural and craft products, the Shakers became economically stable, but their insistence on celibacy required that the community maintain its membership through conversion, a process that inevitably led to their decline.

C. The Oneida Community

This experiment was characterized by a system of "complex marriage" developed by its founder, John Humphrey Noyes. Unlike the Shakers, the Oneidans used sexual freedom to escape the taint of sin. Women were freed from being the property of their husbands, and children were freed from family ties by being communally raised. Of all the socialistic communal experiments, the Oneidans offered the most radical alternative to traditional family life.

D. The Mormon Experience

The Mormon movement was begun by Joseph Smith as a result of visions he experienced in the 1820s. Believing he had been called by God to organize a religious society, Smith combined the ethic of the business class with the organization of a communal society, and the Mormon experience took shape. Growing rapidly in numbers, the Mormons moved from place to place, seeking freedom from persecution and space to establish their earthly Zion. After the assassination of Smith, the Mormons moved to the basin of the Great Salt Lake under the leadership of Brigham Young. There they found the space they needed, and, following Young's directions, they established the most successful of the alternative communities of the antebellum period.

III. The Antislavery Movement

A. African Colonization

One proposed solution to the problem of slavery in America was the return of the slaves to Africa. Northerners who opposed the presence of free blacks in society and southerners who felt that slavery was retarding the economic development of the region formed colonization societies. Although the colony of Liberia was founded on the west coast of Africa, only 1,400 Afro-Americans were relocated there.

B. A Radical Approach

Free blacks vigorously rejected the colonization proposal, insisting that what they really wanted was racial equality and an end to slavery here. In conventions, lectures, and publications, free blacks agitated for the freedom of their enslaved brothers and, in some cases, advocated violent resistance on their part. In 1831, a Virginia slave named Nat Turner organized a revolt against the slaveowners in his area. Along with his companions, Turner killed almost sixty whites, but the local militia quickly ended his bloody rebellion. Whites retaliated by randomly murdering many blacks in the area over the next several days. Turner himself was captured, tried, and hanged, maintaining to the end the appropriateness of his action.

C. Evangelical Abolitionism, to 1840

Some whites, following the lead of free black opponents of slavery, began to call for an immediate end to the institution. These abolitionists argued that the holding of people in bondage was a sin and warned slaveowners that they risked eternal damnation. Perhaps the most vigorous supporter of immediate emancipation was William Lloyd Garrison, the editor of *The Liberator*. He fiercely denounced slaveowners and those who supported them. Another prominent abolitionist was the evangelical minister Theodore Dwight Weld. By publishing *American Slavery As It Is: Testimony of a Thousand Witnesses,* Weld hoped to arouse the conscience of the nation in the interest of abolition. Opponents of slavery used the available forms of mass communication to spread their message among the populace. They also attempted to bring pressure to bear on Congress through petition campaigns. Abolitionism grew in strength during the 1830s but had yet to develop a method that could achieve its goal.

D. Hostility to Abolitionism

In reaction to Turner's rebellion and to abolitionist agitation, the southern states began to enact and enforce stricter codes governing slave activity. A new intellectual defense of the institution as good for the slaves and for society was mounted. Many northerners were sympathetic to the plight of the master class in the South. Opponents of abolitionism in both regions engaged in violent suppression of antislavery activists, and President Jackson publicly supported their efforts to diminish the influence of abolitionism.

E. Antislavery After 1840: The Rise of Free-Soil

Opposition to abolitionism led the Garrisonians to take an even more radical approach, even recommending that the southern states be expelled from the union. A more moderate approach to the problem was expressed in the growing free-soil movement, which sought to prevent the spread of slavery into the western territories. The free-soilers organized politically as the Liberty party and rapidly gained strength among the electorate. Many black abolitionists saw the free-soil policy as the only way to bring the slavery issue into the political arena. In the next decade the Republican party would inherit the free-soil mantle and pursue antislavery goals.

IV. The Movement for Women's Rights

A. Origins of the Women's Movement

The evangelical movement of the 1830s encouraged women to engage in good works. Following this admonition, women became increasingly active in social reform movements, concentrating at first on the plight of single young women but expanding their activities to encompass such problems as prostitution and homelessness. Dorothea Dix led them to become involved in institutional reform, particularly in the quality of care for the insane.

B. Education and Child Rearing

Education attracted the attention of more women than any other aspect of the reform movement. The demand for expanded educational opportunity was widespread, and, under the leadership of Horace Mann of Massachusetts, a standard for public primary school education was established. Women were seen as appropriate teachers for the new schools because they were more stable and had a keener moral sense than the young men they replaced. An enhanced role for women as family educators was also advocated. As child-rearing practices continued to lose their harsh Calvinistic tone, the view of the child as a self-centered but morally educable agent came to the fore. Mothers were urged to devote much of their energy to raising their children properly.

C. Abolitionism and Feminism

Some women rejected the notion that their sphere, however expanded, should be limited to the domestic arena. The Grimké sisters argued that women were equal to men in all respects and that restricting them to the home was the equivalent of "domestic slavery." Not all abolitionist women agreed with the extreme position of the Grimkés, but the opportunities presented by the antislavery crusade brought many women into public life for the first time and in the process antagonized the more conservative clergy in the movement.

D. The Program of Seneca Falls

As women became more active in the abolitionist crusade, they began to consider more closely their own condition in society. Having determined to seek an improvement in women's legal position, they held a convention at Seneca Falls, New York, in 1848. Women's rights advocates continued to meet regularly through the 1850s, and they successfully petitioned state legislatures for an expansion of legal protection for women. Voting rights were not to come, however, even though the movement saw the franchise as the basic right of all citizens. Perhaps the most important result of midcentury feminism was the development of self-confidence and organizational skills on the part of the activists.

ESSAY QUESTIONS

1. Analyze the sources of transcendentalism, and describe its evolution in the thought of Ralph Waldo Emerson.
2. Compare and contrast the philosophy of individualism as it was explored in the literary works of James Fenimore Cooper, Walt Whitman, Nathaniel Hawthorne, and Herman Melville.
3. Discuss and evaluate the ways in which the popular female novelists used the idea of individualism to explore the dilemmas facing American women in the antebellum period.
4. Compare and contrast the communal experiments described in the text—Brook Farm, Oneida, the Shakers, and the Mormons—and examine the strengths and weaknesses of each.
5. Discuss the emergence of the movement advocating the colonization of the slaves. What arguments were mounted in support of this plan? How did free blacks respond to the colonization movement?
6. Describe the emergence of the abolitionist movement and evaluate its plans for eliminating slavery, focusing on the work of Garrison and Weld.
7. Discuss and evaluate the activities undertaken in the North and the South to oppose the abolitionists.
8. What changes in the antislavery movement took place with the emergence of the free-soil policy?
9. How did abolitionism and other reform movements bring women into the public sphere in new ways? How did this development lead women to formulate a new understanding of their role in society?

10. What concrete changes in women's status were achieved as a result of the women's movement in the antebellum period?

IDENTIFICATIONS

William Ellery Channing

American Lyceum

Henry David Thoreau

Moby Dick

Catharine Maria Sedgwick

John Humphrey Noyes

Brigham Young

American Colonization Society

David Walker's *Appeal*

The Liberator

The Grimké sisters

Liberty party

Frederick Douglass

Dorothea Dix

Seneca Falls convention

Margaret Fuller

PRIMARY SOURCE ANALYSIS

"John C. Calhoun Defends Slavery" (p. 389)

1. According to Calhoun, how has slavery benefitted the "black race of Central Africa"?
2. What did Calhoun think was typical in free societies that was missing from the South?
3. What connection can you make between Calhoun's comments on "avarice" in the last paragraph and his defense of slavery?

MAP EXERCISE

"Communal Experiments Before 1860" (p. 381)

1. Why do you think communal experiments were not made in the Deep South?
2. In what ways does this map indicate one of the main differences between the Mormons and the other communal settlements?
3. Which of the communal movements indicated on the map had the largest number of settlements and the widest geographical range?

ILLUSTRATION ANALYSIS

Picture Essay following Chapter 13, Plate 5 (p. 403) and Plate 12 (p. 407)

1. Compare Plates 5 and 12. Both works were commissioned by corporations. But have the two artists suggested a similar relationship between industry and nature?

2. How have the two artists handled the problem of "pollution" that might have been caused by smoke from the locomotives?
3. Is there a church steeple in both pictures? Why do you think an artist might have included this feature in a painting of a factory or a railroad roundhouse?

CHAPTER CONTEXT

The previous chapter described the political impact of Jacksonian Democracy on the expanding business of the 1820s and 1830s.

This chapter explores the emergence of the American literary tradition and the organization of widesprad movements of social reform. Northern writers analyzed the cultural ambiguity of individualism. In reaction to individualism and industrialization, some Americans organized communities designed to foster a cooperative way of life. Opposition to slavery led to the emergence of an abolitionist movement, which drew a violent reaction from proslavery mobs in both the North and South. The free-soil policy of antislavery forces pushed slavery into the political arena. In the cultural chaos of antebellum America, women began to agitate for a larger role in public life. The Seneca Falls convention of 1848 provided an organizational impetus for the women's movement.

The next chapter analyzes the diverging economies of North and South in the 1840s and the increasing sectional tension that this development caused.

14

Social Tension and Sectional Crisis

OUTLINE AND SUMMARY

I. A Distinctive Society

A. The Slave Economy

The southern economy grew rapidly in the decades before the Civil War. Two-thirds of the world's cotton output came from the region. Three factors contributed to this expansion: British markets, fresh land, and slavery. Few immigrants from abroad settled in the South, since they were unwilling to compete with slave labor. The organization of slaves into specialized work gangs made southern agriculture extremely profitable. On the other hand, the concentration on agriculture and the inhuman treatment of the slaves retarded the South's economic development as a self-sufficient modern region.

B. Ideals and Realities of the Planter Class

Although a minority of southerners were slaveowners, their status enabled them to control affairs. In the 1830s they began to foster an image of themselves as noble aristocrats born to rule. The planter's wife shared his exalted image, while in fact she was often a hardworking household manager, responsible for the day-to-day affairs of the plantation. Southern white women were idealized as sexually pure, but the men of the planter class engaged frequently in sexual liaisons with slave women, leading to an increase in mulattoes on the plantations. The racist ideology that proclaimed that all whites are superior to all blacks helped to ensure the loyalty of poorer, nonslaveholding whites. New ideas reached few southerners, and the cultural isolation of the region only increased its antagonism to outside forces.

C. Slave Life

The slaves on prosperous plantations were relatively well clothed and fed in comparison with the poorest whites in the nation. But they remained property and could be bought and sold at will. Expansion of the cotton culture in the Southwest made the working conditions of the slaves there more difficult and increased the dimensions of the domestic slave trade, which further strained the community life of the slaves. Most slaves lived in stable families and developed extensive supportive kin networks. Their religious life, though often clandestine, provided spiritual sustenance and the hope of a better life to come.

D. Resistance and Rebellion

Thousands of slaves sought to escape their plight by running away. Although there was an "underground railroad" of black and white sympathizers, few slaves actually found freedom in the North or Canada. Slaves also resisted the system by destroying property and even on occasion attacking their masters. Violent revolt offered little hope because the master class had too much firepower at its disposal. Planters used poor whites to maintain a reign of terror over the slave population, but masters continued to fear violent slave rebellion. As the antislavery movement in the North gathered strength, southerners saw it as a distinct threat to their treasured way of life.

E. Southern Imperialism

Slaveowners felt that they must have access to the federal territories in the expanding West. They had the support of the government in this quest but worried that if more free states entered the Union they would lose control of Congress. They also feared that Great Britain was trying to establish control over the southwestern boundary of the United States. To prevent this from happening, the South pushed for Mexican territory to be added to the American nation.

II. Accelerating Industrialization in the North

A. Factories Triumphant

The expansion of American industry in the 1840s and 1850s was phenomenal. The widespread use of power-driven machinery and assembly lines in many industries led to a sharp increase in productivity. The invention and application of the stationary steam engine for driving machinery made it possible for factories to be built in already established large cities. No longer dependent on water power, industry was able to take advantage of the larger markets, superior transportation facilities, and growing immigrant population in the cities to increase its output. Increasing production, on the other hand, did not always mesh with increasing demand, and the business cycle of industrial capitalism led to periodic depressions and fluctuating employment patterns.

B. The Buoyant Northwest

By 1860, almost half of America's population lived west of the Appalachians. The Northwest was particularly attractive to settlers, and various federal land acts made it easier to procure good farmland there. The invention and development of new farm machinery—John Deere's steel plow, for example—greatly increased the agricultural output of the Northwest. The spread of the railroad enabled western farmers to get their crops to market and led to the rapid growth of some western cities. The need for iron for the railroads brought about a modernization of the iron industry. Agricultural productivity and efficient transportation made America probably the best-fed nation on earth by midcentury.

C. Business-Class Consumption

Per capita income rose more rapidly in the 1850s than at any other time in American history. The middle class used this increase to purchase larger houses and decorate them. Household implements became commonplace, and inventions such as the sewing machine altered some elements of the domestic economy. The availability of disposable income in the middle class encouraged mercantile developers to establish large department stores in urban areas.

D. Family Planning

Middle-class families began to pay more attention to the welfare of their children. Because of the shift of the family from a producing to a consuming unit, family-planning practices came into play to reduce the number of children, particularly in urban and built-up rural areas. Families remained relatively large, however, compared to those in Europe, because Americans optimistically felt that their children could have fulfilling lives. Due to the high birth rate and to immigration, the American population almost doubled between 1840 and 1860.

E. Immigration

Immigrants, particularly from Germany and Ireland, poured into the United States in the decades before the Civil War. As manufacturers had an increasingly difficult time in disciplining native-born unskilled workers, they turned to immigrants as a prime labor source. The poverty-stricken newcomers were willing to work for less pay and under worse conditions than the American labor force. The living conditions in which the Irish dwelt in eastern cities were deplorable, and urban health hazards led to a series of epidemics that killed thousands.

F. Irish Identity and Anti-Catholicism

The millions of Irish immigrants organized their community life around the Catholic church. Protestants, disturbed by the growing autonomy of what they saw as a "foreign" institution, began an anti-Catholic crusade. This movement was supported by various segments of the population who saw the immigrants as a threat to their way of life and/or their economic security. Political organizations advocated anti-immigrant legislation. Protestant mobs attacked Irish Catholic churches and convents in Boston, and a war broke out in Philadelphia over Bible reading in the public schools. The "Know-Nothing" party met with considerable electoral success in Massachusetts and Pennsylvania in the 1850s, as nativist sentiment increased.

G. Decline of Whig Economics

Although the Whig business-class philosophy appeared politically dominant with the election of Harrison in 1840, the succession to office of Vice-President John Tyler placed Whig politics in jeopardy. Tyler opposed Clay's American System—the centerpiece of Whig policy—and acted more in a Jacksonian economic mode. The Democratic party drew support from immigrant workers and southern farmers and was able to elect James Knox Polk to the presidency in 1844. The Whigs were increasingly divided over the future of the party, particularly over the issue of free-soil. A schism developed between Whigs in the North and South, eroding the party's national base.

III. Party and Sectional Conflict over the West

A. The Texas Rebellion

Americans had carried the cotton culture and slaves into the Mexican province of Texas, ignoring Mexico's laws against slavery. When it appeared that the government of Mexico was on the verge of enforcing its laws in the province, Texans rebelled and sought independence. Supported by southerners rushing to aid them, the Texans defeated the Mexican forces in 1836 and declared Texas an independent republic. They sought immediate annexation to the United States, but their request was delayed by President Jackson because of his fear of further sectional controversy.

B. The Annexation of Texas and "Oregon Fever"

The issue of Texas lay dormant until 1843, when President Tyler joined with southern Democrats to propose a treaty of annexation. Despite their opposition to the treaty, northerners began to link the annexation of Texas with their desire for the United States to claim all of the Oregon Territory. National expansion became the primary issue in the election of 1844, with the Democrats running Polk on a platform to carry American sovereignty to the Pacific and the Whigs running Clay and his American System for what proved to be the last time. The free-soil Liberty party drew enough votes away from Clay to throw the election to Polk. Texas became a part of the United States, and Mexico immediately broke off diplomatic relations.

C. The Mexican War

Polk entered office determined to acquire Oregon and parts of the Mexican lands in the Southwest. The emergent belief in Manifest Destiny rallied support for Polk's expansionist plans. The president secretly sought to enter into negotiations to purchase New Mexico and California and, when Mexico refused, precipitated a military incident that led to the outbreak of the Mexican War. American forces defeated the Mexican army, having advanced all the way to Mexico City. Polk had hoped to annex all of Mexico, but a sharply divided Congress and public opinion required that he settle for the northern portions only. The future of slavery in the Mexican cession was still to be determined.

D. The Wilmot Proviso

During the war, a free-soil Democrat, David Wilmot of Pennsylvania, proposed that Congress bar slavery from the lands to be acquired from Mexico. Although never passed by Congress, this issue provided a rallying point for opponents of slavery and the war. In the election of 1848, free-soil advocates contributed to the defeat of the Democratic candidate, and a Whig general, Zachary Taylor, hero of the Mexican War, was elected. Although Taylor was himself a slaveowner, he was opposed to the extension of slavery into the territories. The election of Taylor and the growing success of free-soil politics made southerners even more determined to win federal support for their program.

E. Slavery in the Territories

Southerners formulated three approaches for expanding slavery into the Mexican cession. Calhoun proclaimed that the federal government had no right to exclude slavery from a territory. Slave property, he argued, was like any other property and could be taken anywhere its owner chose to settle. A more moderate approach called for extending the Missouri Compromise line to the Pacific. While this solution would have certainly added more slave states to the union, it won some support among northern Democrats because it was an attempt at compromise; free-soil advocates, though, opposed any extension of slavery and felt that they had enough power to block either plan. The third policy was "popular sovereignty," a method of leaving the decision to allow slavery or not to the inhabitants of the territory. Each side felt that the ambiguity of this concept had the greatest possibility for maintaining the Union while seeking to obtain the desired results. They were both wrong, as we shall see.

F. California and the Compromise of 1850

When California appealed to join the Union as a free state, the sectional controversy exploded. Southerners saw that the addition of another free state would destroy the balance between their region and the North in Congress and threaten their desired future. Seeking federal guarantees for the future of slavery, southern legislators warned of possible secession if such guarantees were not forthcoming. The intensity of the debate led Congressional leaders to propose the Compromise of 1850, which accepted California's admission as a free state but organized the New Mexico and Utah territories on the basis of popular sovereignty. The compromise also called for the slave trade, but not slavery, to be banned in the District of Columbia and formulated a strengthened federal fugitive slave law. The omnibus bill passed, averting immediate secession, but neither southern Democrats nor northern Whigs were satisfied with the results.

ESSAY QUESTIONS

1. Discuss and evaluate the impact of the cotton culture on the American South.
2. What aspects of the communal life of the slaves helped them develop cultural patterns apart from white society?
3. In what overt ways did slaves seek to escape from the control of the slave system? Evaluate the masters' fear of violent slave uprisings.
4. What industrial developments of the 1840s and 1850s strengthened the interdependence of the East and Northwest? What happened to western cities during this period?
5. In what ways did the middle class begin to turn from a culture of production to one of consumption? How did this shift in values affect family life?
6. Discuss and evaluate the rise of anti-Catholic sentiment during the 1830s and 1840s. In what forms did this sentiment manifest itself?

7. Discuss the political implications of the debate over the annexation of Texas.
8. What factors led to the outbreak of the Mexican War? Discuss the issues in the debate over the peace settlement.
9. In what ways did the Mexican War revive sectional tensions over slavery? What policies did the South advocate to ensure the extension of slavery?
10. Discuss the background of the Compromise of 1850. What were the terms of the compromise? Evaluate the potential of the compromise for resolving sectional conflict.

IDENTIFICATIONS

"cotton kingdom"
domestic slave trade
Harriet Tubman
Samuel Colt
Preemption Act
John Deere
Andrew Jackson Downing
Foreign Conspiracy Against the Liberties of the United States

Know-Nothings
Webster-Ashburton Treaty
Manifest Destiny
"Oregon fever"
Treaty of Guadalupe Hidalgo
"Conscience Whigs"
Wilmot Proviso
Zachary Taylor

PRIMARY SOURCE ANALYSIS

"Advice to Prospective Welsh Immigrants, 1840" (p. 427)
1. Does Chidlaw say that all Welsh immigrants have done well in the United States?
2. What kinds of people are advised not to emigrate?
3. In terms of *social class,* how would you analyze Chidlaw's recommendations to the Welsh on whether they should emigrate or not?

MAP EXERCISE

"Increasing Interior Trade" (p. 423)
1. Comparing this map with the one on page 422, determine what two factors Cincinnati's largest eastern trading partners have in common.
2. With what area does Cincinnati have virtually no trade? Does the map on page 422 tell you why?
3. How would you account for Cincinnati's decreasing trade with some eastern cities in the 1850s?

FIGURE ANALYSIS

"Proportion of Black and White Population" (p. 412)
1. Using the map on page 453, divide the states represented here into three groups: the first seven states to secede, the next five states to secede, and the states that did not secede.
2. What is the approximate average proportion of whites to the total population in each of the three groupings?
3. If you had made a prediction in 1861 about the possible secession of Maryland and Kentucky, which would you have thought more likely to leave the union on the basis of this figure? Why?

CHAPTER CONTEXT

The previous chapter dealt with contradictory attempts to create a stable and moral social order in the midst of the Industrial Revolution.

This chapter explores changes in southern and northern culture that led to increased sectional conflict by the end of the 1850s. Slavery expanded into the Southwest and was defended by the master class as a positive benefit for society. Northern industrialization increased rapidly, particularly in the area west of the Appalachians. On the East Coast, the arrival of large numbers of Irish immigrants led to an anti-Catholic crusade that periodically erupted in violence. Free-soil advocates, growing in strength, were challenging the South's determination to make all federal territory open to slavery. The Mexican War brought the slavery controversy to a head, and the disruption of the Union seemed imminent. The Compromise of 1850 was grudgingly adopted by Congress, and the rift between pro-and antislavery forces was temporarily papered over.

The next chapter will see how the slavery issue finally divided the Union and plunged the nation into Civil War.

15

Two Societies at War

OUTLINE AND SUMMARY

I. The Disruption of Union

A. *The Fugitive Slave Act*

The fugitive slave provision of the Compromise of 1850 prompted the violent confrontation between pro-and antislavery forces. The new act provided for federal support for the return of runaway slaves, guaranteeing slaveowners the security of their "property" everywhere in the Union. Abolitionists began to block enforcement of the Fugitive Slave Act wherever possible, and Harriet Beecher Stowe's *Uncle Tom's Cabin* dramatically portrayed the moral corruption of this federal law. Northern resistance to the act led several southern states to consider secession, but cooler heads prevailed and the South remained in the Union for the time being.

B. *The Disintegration of the Whigs*

The Whig party split over the Fugitive Slave Act. Opposition to the act by the northern wing of the party drove southern Whigs into the Democratic camp in support of the candidacy of Franklin Pierce in 1852. At the same time, many free-soilers believed that the adoption of popular sovereignty had doomed the spread of slavery and thus rejoined the Democratic party. The defeat of the Whigs in 1852 was so severe that they never again waged a national political campaign.

C. Latin American Ambitions

The Pierce administration sought to unite the country through an expansionist foreign policy. In Latin America, southern representatives sought to add Cuba to the Union as a slave state. Pierce at first secretly supported this scheme, but, he backed off when it appeared that a war would be necessary to realize it. When his original intentions became public, northern resentment flared. Another episode involving an attempt to bring Nicaragua into the Union as a slave state also failed.

D. Kansas-Nebraska and the Republicans

Senator Stephen A. Douglas proposed that the northern part of the Louisiana Purchase be organized as the Nebraska Territory, with the slavery issue there to be decided by popular sovereignty. To win southern support, he amended his proposal so that two territories—Kansas and Nebraska—would be formed. This division would would make it possible for southerners to make Kansas a slave territory more easily. The Kansas-Nebraska Act violated the provisions of the Missouri Compromise and put the concept of popular sovereignty to the test. Reaction in the North to Douglas's proposal led to a political realignment. Northern Whigs and free-soil Democrats organized a new party in 1854, calling themselves Republicans. The Republicans' platform was simple—no extension of slavery—and they quickly became a major force in Congress.

E. Republican Ideology Versus the Defense of Slavery

The new party argued that slavery produced only two classes—masters and slaves. This fact, it asserted, distorted the personalities of the members of both classes and precluded their honest participation in the institutions of a free society. Reflecting the ethic of the business class, Republicans asserted that they supported the notion of a classless society of independent, educated, self-reliant citizens. Southerners responded that, to the contrary, a society dominated by a free labor market was bound to be obsessed with greed, the only motive for success in such an economic structure. The South, they contended on the other hand, was a patriarchal, aristocratic society, in which each member had a secure place and all worked together and cared for each other like members of a family. These irreconcilable world views drove the wedge splitting the Union deeper into the heart of the nation.

F. "Bleeding Kansas"

Thousands of pro- and antislavery settlers rushed to Kansas, each side hoping to dominate the territorial legislature. The proslavery group managed to control the territorial legislature with the help of thousands of southern sympathizers from Missouri who crossed the border just to vote. Violence broke out between the two factions in Kansas and thrust the territory and its status into the limelight during the presidential election campaign of 1856. The Republicans nominated the popular John C. Frémont on a platform to stop the spread of slavery by adopting the Wilmot Proviso. The Democrats managed to hold enough northern support to put James Buchanan in the White House. In their first national campaign, the Republicans came within a few votes of gaining political control of the union.

G. The Dred Scott Decision

The Supreme Court rendered the Dred Scott decision after Scott, a slave, had sued for his freedom after having lived for a time in a free state. The Court ruled that no American of African ancestry could be a citizen of the United States and therefore Scott had no right to sue in a federal court. Speaking for the Court, Chief Justice Roger Taney went on to indicate that the federal government had no right to interfere in any way with territorial slavery and that the Missouri Compromise had always been unconstitutional. Buchanan supported the Court's opinion, leading Douglas to break with the administration.

H. Lincoln Versus Douglas

In the 1858 campaign for Illinois's Senate seat, Douglas engaged in a series of debates with Abraham Lincoln, the most prominent Republican in the state. Lincoln attacked slavery as an institution that subverted the basic principles of American democracy. He also attacked Douglas for being a member of the Democratic party, the party of the Dred Scott decision, and for having introduced the Kansas-Nebraska Act. Douglas barely won the election, but the debates had focused national attention on his opponent.

I. The Election of 1860

Southern politicians, desperate now to preserve their region's interests, demanded that the Democratic party protect slavery and even reopen the slave trade. Sectional tension was dramatically increased when abolitionist John Brown led a band of followers into the South in hopes of sparking a massive slave uprising. Defeated and executed, Brown was seen as a martyr by abolitionists and became a symbol for antislavery forces. Southerners became convinced that, if the Republicans gained the presidency in 1860, slavery was doomed. A divided Democratic party could not compete with the unified northern support for the Republicans, and Abraham Lincoln, the latter party's moderate candidate, won the election.

II. Secession and Civil War

A. *The Secession Crisis*

Less than a month after the election of Lincoln, South Carolina seceded, and the "fire eaters" led six more states out of the Union before inauguration day. The secessionists formed the Confederate States of America and elected Jefferson Davis its president. Buchanan tried to hold the Union together but asserted that he had no right to use force to resolve the conflict. In his inaugural address, Lincoln urged reconciliation but stated that secession was illegal and that he would use force, if necessary, to preserve the Union. The war broke out when southerners attacked Fort Sumter in Charleston harbor. Lincoln's call for troops to quell the rebellion drove four more states into the Confederacy. Fortunately, Lincoln's political skills, along with Unionist sentiment, kept the border states from seceding—a factor critical to the success of the northern war strategy.

B. *Military Stalemate, 1861–1863*

The Confederacy had the strategic and emotional advantage at the beginning of the war. It was defending its own borders and struggling for its independence. Somehow the Union had to find the will and determination to pursue its goals. For the first two years, the results of the struggle were inconclusive, except that the Union was able to penetrate the Confederacy and establish critical footholds along the Mississippi River and the southern coast. At several times, one side or the other was close to victory, but inept tactics prevented either from striking the fatal blow.

C. *Lincoln Finds His General*

As the war progressed, it became apparent to Lincoln that to succeed he would have to find a general who would stop at nothing in order to win. He found that man in Ulysses S. Grant. The new tools of warfare in the mid-nineteenth century required a new approach to strategy and tactics. The Civil War was a war of attrition. Massive forces had to be thrown into battle and the other side worn down man by man. With more men to lose, the North was thus likely to win the war, and, accepting the challenge, Grant took over the Union forces.

III. The Northern War Machine and Republican Policies

A. *Mobilization*

In order to wage the total war that proved to be necessary to defeat the Confederacy, Lincoln had to mobilize the North's resources. First, he had to raise an army. A draft was instituted, but this proved to generate more social disorder than troops, and volunteers were recruited with high enlistment bonuses. To finance the war, the government sold Treasury bonds to the public and financial institutions, accepting the necessity of a large deficit. New taxes were levied—including the first income tax—and the average tariff rate was doubled. The war stimulated the national economy in a way that reflected the traditional Whig approach to development. The business class thrived. Railroad companies in particular benefited greatly from federal financial support during the war.

B. Emancipation

As the war went on, Republicans debated the most appropriate manner for emancipation of the slaves. Contrary to Lincoln's plan, some Union generals in the field freed the slaves in areas liberated from the Confederacy. By the middle of 1862, the more radical Republicans and the president agreed that some formal procedure for freeing the slaves should be announced. Released in September 1862, the Emancipation Proclamation freed all slaves in states remaining in rebellion on January 1, 1863. Emancipation was completed when the Thirteenth Amendment was adopted in 1865. As a result of emancipation, more than 200,000 former slaves served in the Union armed forces and contributed significantly to the final victory.

C. The Election of 1864

The campaign of 1864 was a referendum on Lincoln's policies of total war and emancipation. His Democratic opponent, former Union general George McClellan, ran on a party platform calling for an immediate armistice. Lincoln won, aided by the votes of Union soldiers, who supported him by a three-fourths majority.

D. Lincoln's Foreign Policy

Lincoln feared that European nations might help thwart the Union's plans by allying themselves with the Confederacy. Britain's close commercial ties with the South were particularly worrisome. During the war there were several critical incidents that, if strongly reacted to, might have pushed the British into the Confederate camp. Skillful diplomacy averted conflict, however, and the British maintained their neutrality throughout the struggle.

IV. Defeat of the Confederacy

A. Confederate Resources

The Confederates had only one-tenth of the Union's industrial resources, and they never developed an adequate supply of food or clothing for their troops. A smaller population base made it difficult for the South to put as many men in the field as the North could. A lack of capital throughout the struggle seriously hampered the Confederate war effort, and soaring inflation toward the end of the war had an important psychological as well as financial impact.

B. Confederate Leadership

The Confederate states' aversion to centralized government left President Davis without the power to provide firm and effective national leadership. The southern ideologues hoped that appeals to white racial superiority and solidarity would keep their ill-equipped army in the field. Confederate morale cracked in 1863, however, as desertions increased and poor whites began to resent their role in protecting the interests of the planter class. The depths to which the Confederate manpower problem had sunk was exposed in the last months of the war, when the excruciating decision to arm the slaves was made. The war ended, however, before this policy could have any effect.

C. Closing Moves

The North mounted two major campaigns in 1864 that led to the final demoralization and defeat of the Confederacy. Grant's Army of the Potomac engaged Lee's Confederate forces in a long and costly struggle in Virginia. At the same time, General Sherman began his infamous march through Georgia and the Carolinas, destroying everything that stood in his way. Finally, in April 1865, Confederate General Robert E. Lee had no choice but to surrender, and the war came to an end. The Confederacy simply dissolved, and the war-torn South was left in ruins. It remained to be seen how the nation would be able to bind up its wounds.

ESSAY QUESTIONS

1. In what ways did the Fugitive Slave Act contribute to the increasing tension between North and South?
2. What role did Latin America play in American foreign policy during the decades before the Civil War?
3. Discuss and evaluate the ways in which the organization of the Kansas Territory affected the relationship between the free and slave states.
4. Compare and contrast the ideologies of the Republican party and the southern defenders of slavery.
5. How did the Dred Scott decision affect the developing slavery controversy?

6. Discuss and evaluate Abraham Lincoln's attitude toward slavery. What steps did he take to eliminate the institution?
7. Discuss the factors that caused the Confederate states to leave the Union. Trace the historical process involved.
8. Describe the most important campaigns of the Civil War. What strategic developments contributed to the Union victory?
9. In what ways did the Civil War contribute to the development of the national economy?
10. Why did the North win the war? Or, in other words, why did the South lose the war?

IDENTIFICATIONS

Uncle Tom's Cabin
William Walker
"Bleeding Kansas"
Roger Taney
John Brown
"fire eaters"
Jefferson Davis
Fort Sumter

George McClellan
Robert E. Lee
Gettysburg
draft riots
Emancipation Proclamation
"Copperheads"
Sherman's "march to the sea"
Appomattox Courthouse

PRIMARY SOURCE ANALYSIS

"Abraham Lincoln's Gettysburg Address" (p. 459)
1. What major mistake did Lincoln make in his address?
2. Whom do you think Abraham Lincoln is talking about when he uses the words "we" and "our"? Whom does he *not* mean to include? Could his audience have answered these questions with certainty?
3. Is slavery or race mentioned in this address? If not, why not?

MAP ANALYSIS

"The Battle of Gettysburg" (p. 458)
1. Why do you think Stuart's cavalry moved east early in the campaign? Why did Stuart not attack Washington?
2. How many miles did Lee's army cover between May and July 1863? About how much ground could his troops cover in one day?
3. If Lee had won at Gettysburg, what options would he have had? Was he closest to Washington, Philadelphia, or Baltimore?

ILLUSTRATION ANALYSIS

"Lincoln with the Army of the Potomac" (p. 462) and "Grant Planning an Attack" (p. 475)

1. Compare these two photographs of Union headquarters. What do the pictures suggest about the personalities of McClellan and Grant?
2. How many civilians can you count at Grant's headquarters? What do you think they are doing there?
3. How far was Grant from Richmond when the photograph on page 475 was taken? How much time was to pass before Lee's surrender?

CHAPTER CONTEXT

The previous chapter examined the growing split between North and South, focusing on the changing ideology of slaveholding and the emergence of a complex antislavery movement.

This chapter explores the events that led directly to secession and war. The Fugitive Slave Act provoked fierce resistance from abolitionists in the North. The controversy over the Kansas-Nebraska Act led to outbreaks of violence in the Kansas Territory and showed the weakness of the concept of popular sovereignty in border areas. The Republican party emerged out of the political chaos of mid-decade and quickly won control of Congress. The Confederate States of America was formed when the election of Lincoln in 1860 convinced southerners that the only way to preserve slavery was to withdraw from the Union. The bitter and brutal struggle that ensued left, at its end, a defeated and devastated South. In the course of the war, the emancipation of the slaves was begun, and the process was completed in 1865 with the adoption of the Thirteenth Amendment.

The next chapter will describe the course the nation followed in reconstructing itself.

16

The Union
Reconstructed

OUTLINE AND SUMMARY

I. Presidential Restoration

A. Restoration Under Lincoln

Devised while the Civil War was being fought, Lincoln's restoration plan sought to make it as easy as possible for the rebellious states to reenter the Union. His plan called for readmission of a state as soon as 10 percent of its residents who had voted in 1860 took a loyalty oath and agreed to eliminate slavery. Some members of Congress believed that this plan was too lenient and put forth the Wade-Davis bill, which required that a majority of a state's white males swear loyalty to the Union, that slavery be eliminated, and that a new state constitution be written by men who had never supported the Confederacy. The assassination of Lincoln prevented the formulation of a compromise plan.

B. Johnson's Plan for Restoration

President Andrew Johnson, on taking office, announced a policy of restoration similar to Lincoln's, except that it required wealthy southerners to seek a presidential pardon in order to have their rights restored. Johnson had no concern for the welfare of the freedmen. His lack of interest in changing the social system of the South put him on a collision course with radicals in Congress who sought some protection for the ex-slaves. By the end of 1865, all of the former Confederate states were ready to be restored to the Union following Johnson's policies.

II. Congressional Reconstruction

A. Congress Versus Johnson

During the summer and fall of 1865, southern states, recognizing a somewhat sympathetic occupant in the White House, passed a number of laws, known as Black Codes, to assure a continuation of a racial caste system in the South. President Johnson, at the same time, presided over a revival of the Democratic party, seeking to blunt the criticisms of restoration coming from the more radical Republicans.

After hearing testimony about the attempts of southern states to keep the practices of slavery without the institution, Congress sought to protect the rights of the freed slaves by appropriate legislation (the extension of the Freedmen's Bureau, for example). These attempts encountered a presidential veto, however, and the conflict between Congress and President Johnson escalated. Republicans were able to pass a civil rights bill and override the president's veto in early 1866, setting the stage for the important Congressional elections of 1866.

B. The Fourteenth Amendment

In early 1866, the Congressional Joint Committee on Reconstruction submitted the Fourteenth Amendment for consideration. It was designed to guarantee citizenship to the freed slaves and offer them the possibility of voting rights. This amendment became the central issue of the campaigns of 1866 and led to a massive victory for the Republican party. Racial violence against blacks who were trying to participate in Southern politics aided in securing a three-to-one majority for the Republicans in the Congressional elections.

C. Radical Reconstruction and the Impeachment of Johnson

With the power granted by their overwhelming majority in Congress, the Republicans passed the Reconstruction Acts of 1867. These divided the defeated South into military districts and required that a new state constitution guaranteeing black suffrage be written and the Fourteenth Amendment accepted before a state could be considered for readmission to the Union.

In order to stem what they considered to be Johnson's unwarranted interference in the Reconstruction process, Congressional Republicans passed the Tenure of Office Act, which limited presidential control over the removal of officeholders. Johnson's deliberate violation of this act led to his impeachment by the House of Representatives. The Senate failed by one vote to convict the president, but the impeachment process left Johnson without a significant constituency. The Republicans then captured the presidency in 1868 with the election of Ulysses S.

Grant. In the aftermath of an overwhelming victory, the Republicans drafted the Fifteenth Amendment, which said that the right to vote could not be denied on the basis of race, color, or previous condition of servitude. Unreconstructed states were then required to ratify this amendment before being allowed to reenter the Union.

D. The Issue of Women's Suffrage

None of the suffrage legislation during Reconstruction altered the political situation of women. Attempts to ensure the vote for the freed slaves either stated or implied that only males were to benefit. Women who had been active in the abolitionist crusade petitioned, without success, for the vote to be granted to women as well as to formerly disenfranchised men. This failure led to the organization of a feminist crusade for the vote. Some female activists not so directly concerned with suffrage also organized a women's movement that concerned itself with a broader range of gender-related issues.

III. The South During Reconstruction

A. Reconstruction Governments

In their attempts to reconstruct the South, Republicans relied heavily on three groups: blacks, white southerners who had opposed the Confederacy ("scalawags"), and northern whites who had settled in the South after the war ("carpetbaggers"). While blacks played an important role in Reconstruction state governments, they were not dominant. These governments, though accused by southern whites of corruption, actually provided some of the most constructive and progressive administrations the southern states had ever had.

B. The Planters' Reaction

The former slaveowners and their sympathizers allied themselves in an attempt to regain political power in the South. Calling themselves "redeemers," they undertook to overthrow the Reconstruction state governments by whatever means were necessary. Using organized violence, terrorism, and ostracism, they were able to frighten and intimidate both black and white Republicans to stay away from the polls, allowing Democrats to regain political power.

IV. The Plight of the Ex-Slaves

A. Land Reform Fails

The freed slaves hoped that emancipation and a northern victory in the war would provide them with the basis for their economic independence—land ownership. During the war, a few confiscated plantations were turned over to former slaves, thus raising their expectations, but Reconstruction failed to enact a significant land-reform program.

B. Planters Versus Ex-Slaves

The planters, while accepting emancipation, sought to maintain control over their black work force. The ex-slaves, on the other hand, were making efforts to establish independent personal and institutional lives for themselves. The planters continued to use the Black Codes to maintain the racial caste system and control the terms of the blacks' labor. In this effort, they were often assisted by racist federal officials who agreed with the planters that the blacks were fit only for agricultural labor.

C. Sharecropping and Debt Peonage

Because of the planters' lack of capital to pay wages and the blacks' desire to avoid gang labor, sharecropping originally developed as a mutually satisfactory system of agriculture in the postwar South. The inherent possibilities of corruption in the institutions of sharecropping and tenant farming, however, caused many black farmers to descend into debt peonage, from which it became increasingly difficult to escape.

V. The North During Reconstruction

A. A Dynamic Economy

The postwar years saw an immediate increase in northern industrial productivity. Big business got even bigger as the public grew more sympathetic to large-scale enterprise. The growth of extensive rail systems assisted in the opening of the West to settlement and development. Republicans expanded the power of the federal government to promote the development of private enterprise, and a regressive tax system transferred wealth from the poor to the rich, aiding in the process of capital formation.

B. Republican Foreign Policy

While primarily concerned with domestic matters, the government also kept its eye on foreign affairs. Secretary of State Seward had expansionist ambitions. Seeking to acquire American colonies abroad, Seward failed to overcome Congressional opposition to the securing of Caribbean territory, but he did succeed in purchasing Alaska from Russia.

C. The Politics of Corruption

Both Democrats and Liberal Republicans began to challenge the efficiency and honesty of the "spoils system." Clamoring for civil service reform, they attacked the Grant administration for the massive corruption that came to light in the early 1870s. The economic depression of the mid-1870s only heightened the reaction of the public to the scandals, and the Democratic party began to increase its national political power.

D. The Political Crisis of 1877

The Republicans, fearing a Democratic victory in the 1876 presidential election, nominated Rutherford B. Hayes as their candidate. The Democrats countered with a proven corruption fighter, Governor Samuel J. Tilden of New York. Tilden won the popular vote, but a confusion over the legitimacy of electors in certain southern states left the issue of victory in doubt. After much backstage political squabbling, an electoral commission declared Hayes the winner. Since Hayes had promised during the campaign that he would remove federal troops from the South if elected, the one certain development his victory promised was the end of Reconstruction.

ESSAY QUESTIONS

1. Compare and contrast the three different programs for the postwar years: (1) restoration; (2) reconstruction; and (3) redemption. What were their goals, and what policies were adopted in seeking these goals?
2. Discuss the conflicts between Congress and presidents Lincoln, Johnson, and Grant over the course that the federal government was to pursue in the postwar years, with regard to both formulating and enforcing policy in the former Confederate states.
3. Radical Reconstruction provided the best opportunity in the postwar period for establishing racial equality in the South. Describe the policies that worked toward this goal, and evaluate their results.
4. Black people played an active role in establishing an independent life for themselves during Reconstruction. Discuss the significance of the various ways in which blacks sought to create new institutional patterns after emancipation.
5. Indicate the importance of land reform in assisting the freed slaves in their efforts to achieve real freedom during Reconstruction.
6. As the planters began their program of redemption, what actions did they take and how effective were their various policies?
7. Describe the process whereby black sharecroppers and tenant farmers descended into debt peonage.
8. What developments were taking place in the North that deflected the interest of Republicans away from their concern about Reconstruction in the South?

9. What illegal activities by federal officials were uncovered in the 1870s, and what means did political reformers suggest to bring those practices under control?
10. Describe the political conflict that arose as a result of the presidential election of 1876. Discuss the process by which the conflict was resolved.

IDENTIFICATIONS

ironclad oath
Black Codes
Fourteenth Amendment
Radical Reconstruction
Tenure of Office Act
American Equal Rights Association
"scalawags"
"carpetbaggers"

Mississippi Plan
Force Acts
Freedmen's Bureau
sharecropping
debt peonage
"Seward's Folly"
Liberal Republicans
Crédit Mobilier

PRIMARY SOURCE ANALYSIS

"The Mississippi Black Code, 1865" (p. 500)
1. What is the purpose of the threefold designation "freedmen, free negroes, and mulattoes" that is used throughout this source?
2. To what extent were the activities of white people restricted by this statute?
3. What are vagrancy laws? What do the vagrancy provisions of the Mississippi Black Code permit law-enforcement officials to accomplish?

MAP EXERCISE

"The Barrow Plantation" (p. 498)
1. What does the contrast between these two maps tell us about the living arrangements of the freed slaves?
2. Why did the boundary of the plantation change between 1860 and 1881?
3. What do these two maps tell us about the relationship between the planter and the farm workers during and after slavery?

ILLUSTRATION ANALYSIS

"Anti-Republican Sentiment, 1876" (p. 509)
1. Do you think the signs on the wall would actually have been put up in real polling places in the South?
2. What elements of this illustration draw on stereotypes of the period?
3. Does anything about this picture suggest that, if blacks were left alone, they would support their former masters in electoral politics?

CHAPTER CONTEXT

The previous chapter analyzed in detail the events leading up to the Civil War and the course of the war itself.

This chapter describes the struggle between the North and the South over the future shape of the Union and the social structure of the former Confederate states. It compares and contrasts the three conflicting views of postwar policy: restoration, reconstruction, and redemption. Political and industrial change in the North are also introduced, indicating the path the nation was preparing to follow as national leadership turned its attention away from the problems of the South.

The next chapter will explore in detail the continuation of the Industrial Revolution and the changing world of the American working people.